If You *Really* Loved Me...

For one human being to love another: that is perhaps the most difficult of all tasks, the ultimate, the last test and proof, the work for which all other work is but preparation . . . so we must not forget, when we love, that we are beginners, bunglers of life, apprentices in love and must *learn* love . . .

—*Ranier Maria Rilke*

If You *Really* Loved Me...

Identifying and Untangling Love Knots
in Intimate Relationships

by Lori Heyman Gordon

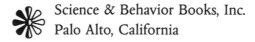

Science & Behavior Books, Inc.
Palo Alto, California

Printed in the United States of America.

Library of Congress Card Number 95-072435

ISBN 0-8314-0086-2

Illustrations by Bob Graham
Printing by Haddon Craftsmen

Dedicated to

VIRGINIA SATIR
*beloved teacher, pathfinder, mentor, friend, who
made this planet a more loving, humane place*

AND

MORRIS GORDON
*my husband, whose remarkable unlimited
vision makes possible the impossible, and
probable the improbable. His encouragement,
patience, and love nurture and sustain me.*

Contents

The Love Knots

The Double Binds

Acknowledgments

This life is a test. It is only a test. If it were a real life, you would have received instructions . . .

—*From a poster (author unknown)*

I am truly grateful to each of you who so openly shared your stories with me of your struggles, your heartaches, your disappointments, your discoveries, and ultimately your joys and triumphs. It has been a privilege to be a part of your lives. I treasure the richness of the adventures we have shared in identifying and changing those knots and binds that sabotage potentially loving relationships. Our many discoveries about assumptions that don't fit, that block the passage to intimacy, have been surprising sources of insight and often even humor. I deeply appreciate you.

I wish to thank my inspiring mentor, the late Virginia Satir, who persuaded me that it wasn't enough to identify and describe the knots—I had to provide the answers. I thank Sheldon Kopp for his original Laundry List, and R. D. Laing for the inspiration of his original *Knots*.

Special gratitude to pioneering marriage and family therapy psychiatrist Clifford Sager, whose insights into the unexpressed, often unconscious expectations that intimate partners have of each other, and that have been inadequately explored, comprise the conceptual base of this book. His sensitive portrayal of couple relationship dilemmas contributed significantly to PAIRS development in making visible the invisible, and explicit the implicit in couple contracting. I am grateful to Bernard Guerney for his penetrating explorations in couple communication and the crucial role that communication skills play in sustaining intimate relationships.

I thank my peers whose enthusiasm, receptivity, and respect for this work launched it into the public domain: Teresa and Jesse Adams, Nancy White, Joe Costanzo, Carl Nissen, Ann Ladd, Shanti Bannwart and Claude Phipps, Carolyn Perla, Marc and Bonnie Rabinowitz, Michelle and Bud Baldwin, Frank Roberts, Frances Bernfeld, and all of the PAIRS leaders who followed. I thank Rita DeMaria, Carlos Durana, Michelle Goss, and Lynn Turner, whose scholarly research papers document the effectiveness of the PAIRS program.

I express appreciation to the Satir IHLRN group with whom I first field-tested my "Laundry List of Marital Mishaps, Knots, and Double Binds" and whose enthusiasm encouraged me to continue; to my Avanta colleagues; to Dr. Israel Charny of Hebrew University in Jerusalem, whose invitation to present at the first Family Therapy Conference in Jerusalem propelled me into identifying and compiling this list; to Gene Waterman, who helped start the initial list; and to the clients, graduate students, and supervisees who joined me in identifying new knots.

I appreciate the encouragement of Diane Sollee, Lyman and Adele Wynne, Paul and Diane Temple, Hara Estroff Marano, Jere Daniel, and the many who interviewed me, sponsored workshops, attended classes, and contributed to spreading these understandings.

Special thanks to Bill and Becky Bestimt, whose perseverance in identifying this collection of love knots enriches this book. Bill claimed the entire collection as "the credo by which I live!"

Special gratitude to Jon Frandsen for his thoughtful editing; to Jerry

D'Amore for his early writing contributions; to Eric Ehrke and Onzie Stevens; to Pat Swift and Cris Cassidy for their extensive help and cheerful goodwill in preparing this manuscript; to Bob and Becky Spitzer, whose early recognition of the significance of the knots and binds encouraged their transition from a list to a book; and to *Science & Behavior* publisher David Spitzer, whose delightful enthusiasm for this material rekindled my own. The list goes on . . .

Loving appreciation to my cherished late parents, Bertha Hahn Heyman and Dr. Julius Heyman. They encouraged my early curiosity, critical and logical thinking, and puzzle-solving. An extraordinary debt of gratitude to my children: Jonathan, David, Beth, and especially my youngest son, Seth, for unlimited patience, love, and encouragement through the years I spent untangling knots. To my dear friend Maybelle Charley, whose devotion, friendship, and commitment to our family made it possible for me to pursue my professional career. And to personal friends whose love and encouragement enabled me to continue the quest when my own spirits flagged: Audrey Glassman, Florence and Paul Dembling, Judy and Stanley Frosh, Betty and Ralph Rothstein, Jean and David Milbradt, Joan Arnold, and Betty Paul.

To our extended families, who add warmth to our lives: my sister Selma, Jon, Barbara, Lisa, Peggy (who invented the *Love Knots* title), Fran, Rob, Ron, Daniel, Albee, Arlene, and Ami. And to our grandchildren: Adam, Benjamin, Sara, Joshua, Lauren, Evan, Alex, Michael, Jessica, Ronny, Donna, and Guy.

To my beloved husband Morris, whose generosity of spirit, humor, patience, and genuine devotion gave me the faith to discover that sustaining a loving relationship is indeed practical reality.

My life has been enriched by each of you. I thank you. I am grateful. May this small volume be a beacon of light and wisdom along life's passages.

—*Lori H. Gordon*

Foreword

The past forty years have seen the coming and going of a large number of marital and/or family enhancement programs. These groups generally have been developed and led by educational, psychiatric, psychological, social work, or religious professionals. Most had their own particular emphasis, depending on the leader's philosophy and beliefs. Almost none had been evaluated in terms of their outcome. Some bordered on cultism or developed into cults. The disparity in their approaches was reminiscent of the adage about the three blind men trying to describe an elephant according to whatever part of the large animal that each happened to be feeling with his hands. Similarly, most of these programs chose one or two areas of focus or ways to attain their objectives.

Ten years ago, I accepted an invitation from Lori Gordon to take her program in the Practical Application of Relationship Skills (PAIRS). A talented and well-trained social worker (who since has earned her doctorate), Gordon had developed this program after being inspired by one of her teachers, Virginia Satir. Satir was a great pioneer who helped develop the specialty of marital and family therapy.

The course has been invaluable to me both professionally and in my personal life. (In the training, professionals take the same program as others do.) Dr. Gordon's genius is clearly evident in her ability to weave together a series of concepts and exercises to resolve interpersonal conflict. Many are her own creation, others are inspired by colleagues. Drawing from the fields of psychoanalysis, psychology, psychiatry, and counseling, she has distilled the essence of their change-producing techniques and organized a new integration that is far greater than the sum of its parts. This synergistic approach helps individuals and couples find change to be relatively easy. It is serious and at the same time fun.

The Book of Untangling Love Knots stands by itself. It is also an example of how Gordon's program works. With clarity and understanding of our foibles, it leads readers into a process that is structured to resolve friction and frustration (with themselves as well as others). Humor and poignancy abound in Gordon's "love knots" and "double binds," which illuminate the many hidden expectations that sabotage our most significant relationships. Currently, the program is in extensive use in this hemisphere as well as in Europe.

Rarely do we read a book whose reverberating impact is capable of changing our lives or those of other people. The contents of this volume suggest a practical, effective way to improve important relationships without blaming or labeling anyone. Nor does this approach provoke guilt or defensiveness. In a sense, it helps us find ways to modify behaviors that may be maladaptive today but that were appropriate earlier in our lives. This open, collaborative process prepares us, as both individuals and couples, to stand tall as we approach the changing world of the twenty-first century.

—Clifford J. Sager, M.D.
Clinical Professor of Psychiatry,
New York Hospital-Cornell Medical Center;
Director of Marital and Family Outpatient Services,
Payne Whitney Clinic

Introduction

"We had everything going for us. How did we get to this?" As a marriage and family therapist, I've spent many years reflecting on the puzzle of how initially loving, apparently intimate relationships so often suddenly founder and capsize. I found this puzzle to be composed of many pieces—pieces that can be sources of misunderstanding and distress in relationships. The pieces formed a complex, rather colorful picture that evolved into my PAIRS (Practical Application of Intimate Relationship Skills) program. PAIRS is now a dynamic, comprehensive, 120-hour course that offers a series of guided exercises focused on those emotions, attitudes, and behaviors that nurture and sustain intimate relationships. It was developed and taught at our PAIRS Institute in Falls Church, Virginia, and elsewhere around the world. Since its beginnings, mental-health professionals from around the globe have trained to lead PAIRS programs.

As I developed PAIRS and investigated the intricacies of relationships, I found consistent, specific sources of trouble. These involve those hidden expectations and assumptions or beliefs that we bring to intimate relationships.

If we are unaware of our hidden expectations or the validity of our differences, they can—with surprising rapidity—sabotage and destroy our relationships. If our life experiences have conditioned us to defend ourselves against the vulnerability involved in love, trust, affection, confiding, closeness, and need, we develop defenses. Tony, a college professor who took PAIRS while well into his second marriage, wrote:

I had such complicated defenses that I couldn't figure out the blueprints myself. The blueprints had been lost years ago and all that was left were the booby traps and fortifications, which had been there so long I thought they were part of the landscape.

The landscape of intimacy is littered with relationships that have been destroyed by hidden expectations and assumptions. Most couples who are unhappy in their relationships feel disappointed, if not outright betrayed, because what they expected to find in the relationship either hasn't happened or has stopped happening. It's as if they believe they had signed an invisible contract early on and their respective partners have failed to honor it. Sometimes, I learned as I conducted the early pairs courses, simply reading and recognizing hidden, unrealistic, or faulty expectations makes it easier to reflect on them and even laugh at and consider changing them.

This book, *If You Really Loved Me . . .* is one result of all of this puzzling. Like the much shorter first edition, it is a somewhat incomplete but often helpful and humorous series of formulas designed to bring to the surface your hidden expectations of yourself and your partner. Awareness and reflection are powerful tools. It is my wish that this little book will help you to take that pause that will lead to new understanding, acceptance, and peace of mind.

May the list of knots and binds and the accompanying Dialogue Guide help you to avoid some of the pitfalls and find more of the pleasure possible between loving partners.

What Happened?

It happens to everyone. A simple caress that is intended to comfort or please feels like an intrusion. You flinch or recoil, as you would from a sudden and searing electrical shock. You tell him to stop. Or you reach to hug your lover, and he behaves as if he were being sucked into a cyclone, yanking away without a word.

Sometimes such responses are a simple anomaly, a result of being worried or scared or simply out of sorts. But all too often such encounters become more frequent. They begin to snowball. The house slowly divides into his-and-her territories, with the kitchen and bathroom serving as demilitarized zones. The bedroom is an awkward Twilight Zone where truces are called and broken over and over. The thoughts during such times—sometimes spoken, sometimes kept hidden—are simple, sharp, and indisputable commands, ranging from a whispered and pained "Just leave me alone" to a furious "Go to hell!" But when the enemy is gone and the threat has receded, you have time to think, not just react. Maybe you recall how much you once loved to be touched by Susan or Jim and wonder how that same gesture came to be frightening, something that threatened to restrain or hurt rather than comfort. You may even fantasize about being held and stroked by a nicer version of your partner—the one you fell in love with, not the one you live with now. And maybe you just sit in the dark and let your brain shout one question, the question you might never ask the person with whom you share your life: "What happened?"

What happened is that you've been bumping into love knots and the even more tortuous double binds. But we lack the knowledge to understand and then unravel them and we fall back on what we *do* know. We know we are withdrawing, either by shrinking away in pain from our partners or by chasing them off in anger. We know we just want to be away because our partners make us feel angry or hurt. But even though we try and try, we never arrive at an answer. Weary of the pondering, fuming, fretting, and struggling, we eventually shrug it off with a "Who knows" and cope as best we can, either by letting the situation perpetuate or by leaving. We give up.

WHAT'S A LOVE KNOT?

A love knot is caused by subconscious assumptions—about love, about families, about what we can and cannot talk about—that we bring to our intimate relationships. It tends to act like a landmine: if touched, it explodes. It erodes relationships.

Although many of these beliefs and expectations we have about love, relationships, and marriage originate in childhood, we accumulate and alter them throughout our lives, all the while keeping them hidden not only from our partners but generally from ourselves. These beliefs usually burst into our conscious mind only when we feel hurt, frightened, or disappointed. Then our minds are so scrambled by these emotions that we cannot see clearly, evaluate them logically. We act on these vague "rules" and expectations anyway and react when someone violates them, even though many of them are faulty.

Many love knots have to do with what we want and what we expect from our partners. Among the most common of these is: "If you really loved me, you would know what I think, what I need, or what I feel." Many partners are astonished—and hurt—when we do not know that they are upset, or why. They might say to us, "Well, if you don't know . . ." and walk off, leaving us puzzled or even feeling vaguely guilty. Implicit here is the belief that if someone loves you, they know what's in your mind and heart and have an instinctive regard for your likes and dislikes. And if they do not know, then they must not love you, which is why you get angry or hurt and walk away or lash out. Unfortunately, this belief is deeply flawed. The only way to know for sure what someone wants or cares about is to be told. You must make your expectations explicit. To expect your partner to read your mind is to court disaster.

Another cluster of unhealthy assumptions has to do with expressing feelings. "If I tell you how I feel, you will be angry. I am afraid of your anger, so I can't tell you." Or "If I tell you how I feel, you will be upset. I can't stand how I feel when you are upset, so I live a lie." (This particular belief often leads to relationships based more on a distorted form of etiquette than love. One person is so fearful of hurting the other by saying honestly that their feelings of love have diminished, that they stay, all the while growing more disappointed and even bitter.) Underlying this set of assumptions is the all too common but dead wrong belief that we are responsible for how our partners feel. We are not. We are responsible for our own behavior and the way we express ourselves. We certainly can avoid behaving in a hurtful manner or speaking in a nasty way, but we cannot prevent those close to us from experiencing pain, fear, and anger. What we can do is listen when our partners want to express those feelings. Talking through the feelings allows them to diminish, and provides the information we need to discuss what caused the pain, fury, or fear. Then we can determine whether anything can be done about the cause.

We rarely ask ourselves why we expect certain things or particular behaviors from the people we love. If we did, we might be surprised at some of the unfair demands we unconsciously make on them. And we might be surprised that we can indeed figure out "what happened." There are answers, and frequently the answers give us the tools we need to revive a relationship we desperately would like to count on and preserve. Identifying the hidden expectations each of us brings to a relationship is an important step toward resolving or warding off misunderstandings and disappointments.

We expect things of our intimates that we expect of no one else. Our expectations become the basis of a private litmus test we constantly apply to our lovers. They flunk when we experience a bewildering feeling of betrayal, when we realize that what we expected is not what our partners expected or are even capable of fulfilling.

The first key to finding out "what happened"—to avoiding or banishing the alienation that tears apart many relationships—is ferreting out from our subconscious this list of faulty assumptions and expectations: the love knots that bind us together in pain instead of pleasure and love. Once we identify these knots, we can untangle them and learn to replace frustration and confusion with healthier expectations for and beliefs about love that allow us to grow closer together, not run away.

DETECTING THE LANDMINES

Read through the love knots and double binds in a thoughtful way. Don't be surprised if you find some of them upsetting. They may include beliefs so deeply embedded that you may find it difficult to believe they aren't simply truths. It may be difficult to imagine giving them up. Many of these expectations are attitudes we developed while we were growing up, when other people controlled our lives and when we were attempting to define, make sense of, and sometimes protect ourselves from the baffling behavior of adults. As you spot ones that fit, remember that they are worthy of respect; they helped you to cope with an ever-changing world. But now that we have greater control in our lives, we can develop new ways of coping that allow us to explore its joys and secrets with fewer restraints.

Each love knot and double bind is illustrated with a scenario, showing the havoc a particular belief or expectation might cause. Each love knot also has a corresponding "unknotted" attitude that can be used to gently nudge out of the way the more self-defeating attitudes we carry with us. And there is a scenario showing how different the results can be when we are aware of our knots and binds.

Pay particular attention to the love knots and double binds that feel familiar. Use the scenarios to help you reconstruct situations where the knots may have hampered your relationship with a lover, family member, close friend, or even a colleague at work. Using the unknotted attitudes and scenarios, think through alternative ways in which you could handle these situations.

Love knots are habits of thinking so deeply ingrained that they become subconscious. They evolve from our earliest experiences and often are tied to deeply emotional events in our lives. The last section of this book discusses how we absorb these events, react to them, and carry them into relationships. Being aware of how the past haunts the present is a potent tool for having a more conscious, deeper, and joyful relationship, but there are other things that interfere with our happiness as well. In addition to sometimes unrealistic expectations and damaging attitudes, we also develop *styles* for expressing those expectations and attitudes. During emotionally charged moments, these styles come to the fore with a fury. Unfortunately, they often hinder our ability to be clear and forthright. Instead, our attempts to tell someone how unhappy we are collapse into fights that further aggravate the situation. The Dialogue Guide and other tools for communication in the last section can help in both untangling knots and binds and to clearly express your concerns.

Exploring these knots and binds is a necessarily difficult voyage. By reconsidering our most basic beliefs about love and the people we love, we are digging into the most vulnerable parts of our psyche. Naturally, this can be unsettling and even upsetting. While discomfiting, this is a sign that you are delving into areas that matter deeply. As this happens, recall that these knots developed as a way to cope with your world. They served you well during that time, just as a child's sneakers protected your feet and took you where you wanted to go. But your feet are larger and your world is different now. New attitudes—new shoes—will serve you equally well now, allowing you to live with fewer restraints and to walk with sure footing.

The Love Knots

1. If You Really Loved Me . . .

THE LOVE KNOT

If you really loved me, you would know what I want, and
you would do it.

Since you don't, you obviously don't care.

So why should I care for you, or for what you think, feel,
say, want, or do? When you tell me what you want, I
won't be very interested. I will be withholding.

UNTANGLING THE KNOT

I cannot assume that you know. I will ask for what I want
and not expect you to know.

THE SCENE

Pat: How was your day?

Chris: Fine.

Pat: Good.

Chris: [*Thinks*] Can't you tell how hurt and angry I am? You always ask how I am, but you don't really want to know. If you don't care, I'm not going to tell you. In fact, I don't want to tell you anything!

THE REWRITE

Pat: How was your day?

Chris: Lousy. You forgot our anniversary. The kids have been obnoxious, and I feel like everybody in my life is grabbing for a piece of me. I just want peace and quiet.

Pat: I thought it was tomorrow! I'm sorry. I wish I could put the kids on loan for a week and get away with you. But how about if I just hold you and tell you how good it makes me feel to find you here when I get home? We'll do something special tomorrow, okay?

9

2. The Evening News

THE LOVE KNOT
If you really loved me, you would talk to me.
You don't.
You don't really love me.

If you really loved me, you would listen to me.
You don't.
You don't really love me.

UNTANGLING THE KNOT
Perhaps you're not a talker. Perhaps you are preoccupied.
Perhaps you never learned to talk (or listen). I will check
out my perceptions and not assume.

THE SCENE

Lou: [*Sits, reading the paper and watching the news on TV*]

Sandy: I wish you'd put down the paper and talk to me. I've had a lousy day, and I'd really like you to keep me company.

Lou: [*Ignores Sandy and continues to read*]

Sandy: [*Leaving*] There's no point in trying to talk to you. Forget it.

THE REWRITE

Lou: [*Sits, reading the paper and watching the news on TV*]

Sandy: I wish you'd put down that paper and talk to me. I've had a terrible day, and I'd really like you to keep me company.

Lou: Come sit by me. I'll be through in a few minutes, and then I want to hear about it.

Sandy: [*Snuggling up*] Okay.

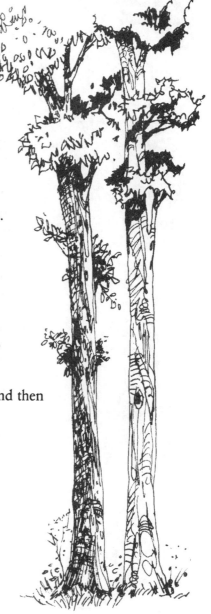

3. It's My Style

THE LOVE KNOT
If you really loved me, you would agree with me.
You don't. You don't really love me.
If you really loved me, you would want what I want and
like what I like.
You don't. You don't really love me.
If you really loved me, you would not try to change me.
You try to change me. You don't really love me
(for who I am).

UNTANGLING THE KNOT
We are all unique. We are all different. Agreement doesn't
necessarily indicate love, nor does disagreement necessarily indicate lack of love.
We can discuss our differences, understand them, change
them, or accept them.

THE SCENE

Shawn: I like that contemporary look. Let's get Scandinavian chairs for the dining room.

Terry: I hate contemporary. I like antiques. I'd rather get Italian Provincial.

Shawn: That's too expensive! And uncomfortable! I hate that stuff.

Terry: You never want anything I want. I'm sick of arguing over every little thing. Why does it always have to be your way?

THE REWRITE

Shawn: I like that contemporary look. Let's get Scandinavian chairs for the dining room.

Terry: We're different that way. I like antiques. I want Italian Provincial.

Shawn: They're so expensive. And they're uncomfortable for me.

Terry: Well, I can go for contemporary style in the dining room, if you can live with Italian Provincial in our bedroom. I prefer that style. I'd rather wait for it.

Shawn: It's a deal.

4. Take Me Away

THE LOVE KNOT
If you loved me, you would bring excitement and new experiences into my life. You would plan them and make them happen.
You don't.
You must not feel I am worth doing that for.
You don't love me.

UNTANGLING THE KNOT
Part of our uniqueness is that we are drawn to different things. I must take responsibility myself for making happen what I would like to have happen, and not see your initiative as a test of my worth.

THE SCENE

Max: I'm tired of sitting around here all the time. All you ever want to do is read or vege out in front of the TV.

Billy: Well, I need peace and quiet. It relaxes me.

Max: [*Thinks*] What happened to the lover who brought all that excitement and laughter into my life? Things are so boring now—and so are we! [*Says*] It sure makes you dull to be around.

Billy: Thanks a lot. I didn't know I'd signed up as your chief entertainer.

THE REWRITE

Max: I'm tired of sitting around here all the time. All you ever want to do is read or vege out in front of the TV.

Billy: Well, I need peace and quiet. And I like sharing it with you.

Max: I like it, too, but I get restless sometimes. I need to get outside. I think I'll go for a hike Sunday. Want to come?

5. Ugly Duckling

THE LOVE KNOT
If you loved me, you would find me attractive. You would
tell me so. You would want to be close to me.
You don't. You don't love me.

UNTANGLING THE KNOT
When you don't appear to find me attractive, I cannot
assume I know why. I will ask for the information I
need, check out my perceptions, and not assume
(ass-u-me—i.e., if I assume anything, it can make an
ass out of you and me).

THE SCENE

Robin: [*Thinks*] You've been so distant recently. It doesn't feel as if you still love me. [*Says*] I wish you'd stop treating me like a piece of furniture.

Gerry: Huh? What are you talking about?

Robin: Just what I said. I'm sick of feeling ignored.

THE REWRITE

Robin: It feels like you haven't paid much attention to me recently. I'm starting to feel like you're not attracted to me anymore.

Gerry: I've been working hard recently. I guess I've forgotten to let you know how much it means to me to have you here—how just looking at you makes me feel better.

6. Thanks for the Memory

THE LOVE KNOT

If I were important to you, you would remember what I tell you.

You don't. You don't think what I have to say is important.

You don't think I'm important. You don't love me.

UNTANGLING THE KNOT

My expectations are unrealistic. Even when you listen, you may be distracted or preoccupied, or you may forget. If what I want you to hear and remember is important, I need to make you aware of that. I also need to get your full attention. Your ability to remember is not necessarily a reflection of your feelings for me. When I'm in doubt about your feelings, I will ask and not assume.

THE SCENE

Dale: Well, I'll see you in a week, when I get back from Tulsa.

Lee: What do you mean?

Dale: You know, my annual convention. I'm leaving tomorrow.

Lee: Oh. Maybe you told me, but I forgot.

Dale: [*Angrily*] Don't you ever listen to what I tell you?

THE REWRITE

Dale: Well, I'll see you in a week, when I get back from Tulsa.

Lee: What do you mean?

Dale: You know, my annual convention. I'm leaving tomorrow.

Lee: Oh. Maybe you told me, but I forgot.

Dale: How could you forget? Does that mean you don't care what I say?

Lee: No, silly. I'll miss you a lot, and I guess I didn't want to think about not being able to see you for a week. Will you call me?

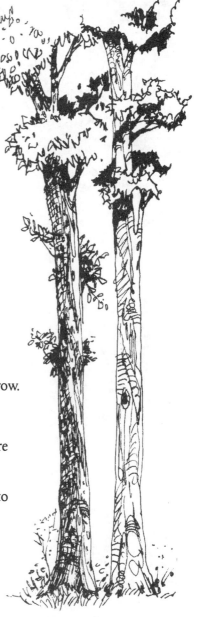

7. The Birthday

THE LOVE KNOT
If I were important to you, you would remember special
anniversaries, our special dates and times.
You don't. I'm not important to you.
You don't love me.

UNTANGLING THE KNOT
When you don't remember these events, I will let you
know their importance to me. I will tell you of my hurt,
disappointment, or resentment. If you choose to ignore
what is important to me, our relationship will surely
suffer. We need to develop a relationship in which each
of us feels loved and valued.

THE SCENE

Angel: Isn't your birthday this month?

Kim: [*Coldly*] Yes.

Angel: When?

Kim: Last Tuesday.

Angel: Thanks for telling me! Why didn't you say
something?

Kim: Never mind.

THE REWRITE

Kim: This is my birthday.

Angel: Thanks for telling me! Why didn't you say
something?

Kim: You know, I'm hurt. When you don't take the trouble to
keep track, it's like you don't care about my feelings.

Angel: Sit down with me while I get out my datebook, and I'll
write it down for the future. And let's go out for a belated
celebration!

8. Home Alone

THE LOVE KNOT
If you tell me what you want, I feel controlled or
obligated to do what you want. When I feel controlled,
I feel weak and inadequate.
I cannot give you what you ask for without
feeling resentful.

If you tell me your feelings, I *must* do what you want.
That would interfere with what I *want [think, feel, am doing]*.
So I don't want to hear or know your feelings.

UNTANGLING THE KNOT
I need to be able to relate my feelings, and I need to be
able to hear yours. Neither of us is obligated to do
anything about each other's feelings.

THE SCENE

Sasha: I felt really lonely tonight while you were out.

Jay: Stop trying to make me feel guilty. What am I supposed to do, cater to your every whim?

Sasha: There's no point in trying to talk to you! Forget I said it!

THE REWRITE

Sasha: I felt really lonely tonight while you were out.

Jay: I haven't seen Sue in more than a month, and she really means a lot to me.

Sasha: I know. I didn't mean you should have been here. I just wanted you to know that I miss you when you're not here!

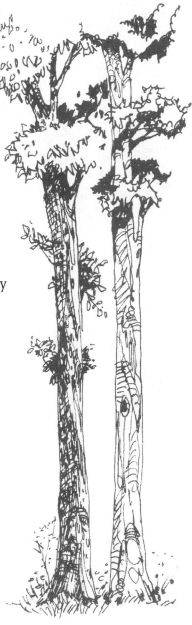

9. Stingy Santa

THE LOVE KNOT
If I give to you and you don't acknowledge it, I feel unappreciated.
Since what I give you is unappreciated, I will be withholding.

UNTANGLING THE KNOT
It is important to take pleasure in knowing that I am giving, without waiting to be acknowledged.

THE SCENE

Ernie: [*Lies in bed, sick*] Could you get me some orange juice before you leave?

Rhett: You know, I've been waiting on you hand and foot for the past week, and you don't even say thank you.

Ernie: I didn't know I was so much trouble. Why don't you just leave? I'll get it myself.

THE REWRITE

Ernie: Could you get me some orange juice before you leave?

Rhett: Sure. But I need to tell you, I'm getting worn out. I hope you feel better soon.

Ernie: Me too.

10. The Gilded Chain

THE LOVE KNOT

If I acknowledge how much you do for me, I feel
beholden, burdened, and obligated to do for you.
So I cannot acknowledge what you do.
You feel unappreciated.
You distance.

UNTANGLING THE KNOT

Expressing appreciation for what you do is an important
part of sustaining love. No one is obligated to return a
lover's favors—that is a personal choice. I can appreciate
what you do for me without being in your debt.

THE SCENE

Marty: Here's some orange juice. I hope you feel better. Do you need anything else?

Pat: [*Thinks*] Boy, when I'm better, you're going to want all kinds of payback. [*Says*] Quit hovering around me. It makes me feel like a child.

Marty: Fine! That's the last time *I'll* offer.

THE REWRITE

Marty: Here's some orange juice. I hope you feel better. Do you need anything else?

Pat: Just to let you know I love all this attention. I feel so rotten. It's the only thing that makes me feel better.

Marty: I'm glad. I was hoping I could help.

27

11. Heavyweight Champ

THE LOVE KNOT
If we don't agree, one of us must be wrong.
If it is me, that means I am bad, stupid, ignorant,
or inadequate.
So it can't be me.
I must prove that it is you, so I won't feel like a failure.

UNTANGLING THE KNOT
We should be able to disagree.
We are all unique, and disagreements are manifestations
of our uniqueness.

THE SCENE

Terry: Boy, was that a stupid movie, or what?

Leigh: I liked it.

Terry: How could you like it? Everything was so obvious. You'd have to be an idiot to like it.

Leigh: You probably didn't understand it. Maybe you're the idiot!

THE REWRITE

Terry: Boy, what did you think of that movie?

Leigh: I thought it was pretty interesting. I enjoyed it.

Terry: Really? I was kind of bored. What did you like about it?

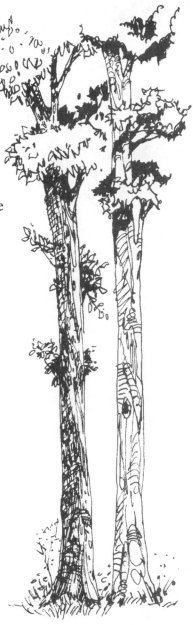

12. Keeping Up with the Joneses

THE LOVE KNOT
If you are more successful, more competent than I am, I
feel diminished and put down.
I distance from you.

UNTANGLING THE KNOT
It is only useful to compare myself with myself: with
where I have been, what I am learning, and what else I
want to accomplish. Comparing myself with another
evokes envy, jealousy, and feelings of competition. We
are all struggling to survive and grow, and to use
the opportunities that life offers. To sustain intimacy,
we need to be able to offer each other mutual support
and encouragement.

THE SCENE

Chris: You won't believe it. I made two more sales this afternoon.

Marty: [*Thinks*] Geez, there you go again, talking about how great you are. [*Says*] That's great. I'm going out for some groceries.

Chris: I'm glad it's so important to you! What's with you, anyway?

Marty: I have better things to do than stand here and massage your ego.

THE REWRITE

Chris: You won't believe it. I made two more sales this afternoon.

Marty: Geez, that stuff is really taking off. You're doing so well, I'm jealous. I'm stuck at my job, and seeing things happen for you makes me feel twice as bummed. Maybe I should think about changing jobs.
Meanwhile, where are you taking us to celebrate?

Chris: Where shall we go?

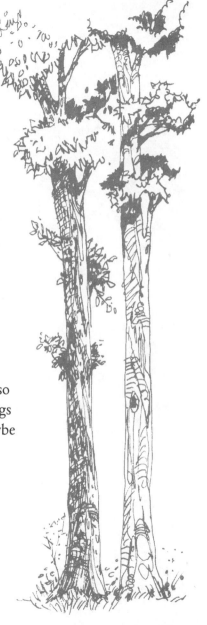

13. Masquerade

THE LOVE KNOT

If I tell you how I feel, you will be angry. You will attack me or withhold from me.
I am afraid of your anger and your distance.
I can't tell you.
I live a lie.

If I tell you how I feel, you will be hurt.
I can't stand how I feel when you are hurt.
I can't tell you.
I live a lie.

UNTANGLING THE KNOT

We need to be able to risk confiding our feelings, and to listen with understanding and empathy. I need to be able to listen to your feelings, consider them, and discuss them. It is destructive to act out my feelings by withholding, attacking, or distancing from you.

THE SCENE

For months, Linda has had growing doubts about her changing feelings toward Tom. She cares for him and doesn't want to hurt his feelings. She behaves as if everything is okay, but she is acting. The more she pretends everything is fine, the more hollow she feels.

THE REWRITE

Linda: Something is happening that we need to talk about. I care for you, but something's missing. I feel like I'm falling out of love with you.

Tom: Boy, that knocks the wind right out of me. I thought everything was fine. What's missing?

Linda: I don't know. That's what bothers me. Maybe things might get clearer if we talk.

Tom: Okay. Want me to listen or to ask you questions?

14. The Judge

THE LOVE KNOT

If I tell you how I feel, you interrupt, disagree, give advice, judge, or dismiss my feelings. I stop telling you. I distance.

UNTANGLING THE KNOT

If I want you to listen to me and to hear me without comment, I have to ask for that.

It is not a gift to give advice or comments when the other person does not want or ask for them. We need to be able to listen for information and deeper understanding.

Listening is a most important gift to a relationship.

THE SCENE

Shawn: Hey, I'm upset. Someone ran into me in the parking lot at lunch. We had to call the police!

Darryl: I knew this would happen. You don't look where you're going. You'll probably lose your license. Did you call a lawyer?

Shawn: I don't need a lecture. I'm sorry I even told you. What makes you think you're so smart, Know-It-All?

THE REWRITE

Shawn: I'm upset. Someone ran into me going out of the parking lot. We had to call the police.

Darryl: [*Putting arms around Shawn*] Are you okay? Was anyone hurt? How's the car?

Shawn: I feel awful. The damage isn't too bad. No one was hurt, but I hate that this happened. Thanks for understanding.

35

15. The Handyman

THE LOVE KNOT

If you are in pain, I believe I should be able to fix it.
I don't know how to fix it, so I feel inadequate.
I get angry at you for making me feel inadequate. I
withdraw from you and blame you when you are in pain.

UNTANGLING THE KNOT

When I am in pain, what I want is interest, comfort,
empathy, sympathy, an interested ear, to be listened to—
not solutions. As an adult, I have my own intelligence and
can figure out solutions for myself. If I want advice or
help, I can ask for it.

When you are in pain, I can be supportive without
believing I have to provide a solution. I can listen,
empathize, and acknowledge what you say— even how
I feel about hearing it. I will respect and honor your
feelings as well as your ability to ask for what you want.

THE SCENE

Billy: I blew up at work today. I may have lost my
job. I think I'm falling apart!

Alex: [*Thinks*] I don't know how to help. [*Says*] That's
just like you, to lose your temper. You're jeopardizing
everything we have, you know.

THE REWRITE

Alex: I blew up at work today. I may have lost my job.
I think I'm falling apart!

Billy: That's terrible. Come here, let me hold you . . . we can
talk about it later.

16. Perfecto the Indestructible

THE LOVE KNOT
If *I* were what I should be, I would never be weak, tired, impotent, afraid . . . [*add your own adjectives of inadequacy*].
But I am.
Therefore I feel inadequate.
I must hide my feelings so you won't find out how inadequate I really am.
I live a lie.

UNTANGLING THE KNOT
All of us have times when we feel badly. Hiding my feelings from you keeps us strangers. Sharing my feelings brings me closer to you.
Sharing my feelings helps you be able to confide your feelings to me.

THE SCENE

Val: [*Is worried about work deadlines, bills, and health*]
   Hi.

Tony: How are you?

Val: Fine.

Tony: You look tired.

Val: I'm okay.

THE REWRITE

Tony: How are you?

Val: I've got a lot on my mind. I'm exhausted, losing sleep
   over that report, and I don't want to risk losing this
   job. We can't afford it.

Tony: I know how hard it is. I'm sorry.

17. On Your Own

THE LOVE KNOT
If I were what I should be, *you would be* happy.
I would be able to solve [fix] everything.
Since I can't, your unhappiness makes me feel inadequate,
guilty, and angry—at you.
I distance myself from you.

UNTANGLING THE KNOT
I cannot solve or fix everything for you. No one can do
that for another. I cannot take responsibility for your
happiness. Each of us must do that for ourselves. I can
show you that I care.

The Scene

Jay: [*Returns from a counseling session about the recent death of her father and problems concentrating at work*] I'm upset. I feel sad all the time.

Sheridan: [*Angrily*] I don't want to hear about it. I'm tired of you moping around. This house is a mess.

The Rewrite

Jay: I'm upset. I feel sad all the time.

Sheridan: Ever since you've been seeing that counselor, I've felt left out. Like you don't need me any more.

Jay: That's not true. I need you. But I need a counselor to help me sort out some things about my dad dying. It doesn't have much to do with you. I have to work this through myself.

Sheridan: Oh. Well, I'm glad you told me. Thanks.

18. The Nerve!

THE LOVE KNOT
If I don't allow you to know my feelings, I resent your complaining about yours.
I resent you doing what I won't allow myself to do.

UNTANGLING THE KNOT
Intimacy and trust build as I allow you to know me. The bond between us builds by our sharing a range of feelings—including pain, sadness, fear, anger, excitement, humor, joy, pleasure, and love. Then nurturing the pleasure of intimacy that is possible between us.

THE SCENE

Sandy: [*Thinks*] I had a lousy day. I got through it, but I'm gonna crash when I get home.

Brooke: [*As Sandy comes in*] How are you, hon?

Sandy: Great! How are you?

Brooke: Terrible!

Sandy: Aw, for crying out loud. Can't you let me get in the door before you start whining? [*Thinks*] Who the hell are you to complain? I never complain, for godsake.

THE REWRITE

Sandy: [*Thinks*] I had a lousy day. I got through it, but I'm gonna crash when I get home.

Brooke: How are you, hon?

Sandy: Awful! I need a hot bath, a drink, and a backrub. You up to it? By the way, any mail?

Brooke: Here it is. I'll run you a hot bath. I may even get in with you. I'm exhausted, too. Let's just relax for a while. I might be able to rub your back after I unwind.

19. Twelve Steps

THE LOVE KNOT

If you were what you should be, you would never be *sad, angry, bored, boring, worried, suspicious, tired, loud, sick, selfish, weak, disagreeable, clumsy, controlling, flirtatious, or demanding* [add your own adjectives of imperfection and inadequacy]. You are.

I feel cheated, betrayed. I distance myself from you.

UNTANGLING THE KNOT

We are all different ways at different times. We each have many sides. We need to accept this in ourselves and each other, and discuss what we need each other to change.

The Scene

Abbie: You were such a bore at that party last night. You sat in the corner, didn't talk to anyone, and then fell asleep on the couch and snored! I was so humiliated. I don't want to go anywhere with you!

Lee: Quit nagging me.

The Rewrite

Abbie: What happened to you last night? You sat off in the corner, fell asleep, and snored. I was really embarrassed.

Lee: Sorry. I was exhausted. I didn't sleep much the night before. I've had that project on my mind.

Abbie: I didn't realize. You know, when you're that tired, it would be okay with me if we didn't go. Just let me know. I'd rather not go than have you fall asleep.

20. If Only

THE LOVE KNOT
If you were what you should be, I would be *happy, successful, popular, attractive, virile, potent, sexy* [add your own adjectives of appeal and desirability].
I'm not.
It's your fault.

UNTANGLING THE KNOT
No one can make another person anything. Each of us needs to develop the talents, abilities, and qualities we desire in ourselves.
I can ask my partner for help, but the responsibility for my destiny remains my own.

THE SCENE

Tommy: I got passed over for promotion.

Alex: That's too bad.

Tommy: You know, I might have made it if you had supported me—if you had been nicer to my staff, entertained, and pushed me to exercise and stay in shape.

THE REWRITE

Tommy: I got passed over for promotion.

Alex: That's too bad.

Tommy: I've been thinking about what I could do differently in the future. I think I'd be nicer to my boss, entertain the staff, and lose weight. I'd appreciate it if you'd help me. Maybe I'll make it next time.

Alex: I'm with you.

47

21. Not Me

THE LOVE KNOT

If you say you love me, you either don't know me, want to use me, or are stupid and have poor judgment.
I can't love you.

UNTANGLING THE KNOT

Life has risks. Relationships have risks. Our choice is risking versus simply existing—without either disappointment or pleasure. I will never know the outcome that our relationship can have unless I risk it.

As an adult, I have my own resources. I am not helpless, even when I am disappointed. I need to be able to risk letting you know me, to check out my perceptions, and to accept that I am lovable and good enough. And if you love me, you have very good judgment!

THE SCENE

Kelly: The first couple of times we went out, we had a terrific time, and I told you how much you were starting to mean to me. Right after that, you seemed to pull back.

Morgan: Relationships and me never work out. I guess I'm just a loner.

Kelly: I'm really sorry to hear that.

THE REWRITE

Kelly: The first couple of times we went out, we had a terrific time, and I told you how much you were beginning to mean to me. Right after that, you seemed to pull back.

Morgan: Look, sometimes I get scared of being hurt again. I think I don't ever want to be involved in another relationship. I look at you and wonder, "If you get to know me, that would be the end . . ."

Kelly: Well, so far, things have been pretty good—terrific, as a matter of fact. Besides, I'm probably just as scared as you are. I'm just more scared of letting fear dictate my life.

Morgan: I'll give you credit for being honest. Keep talking . . .

22. Hair Shirt

THE LOVE KNOT
If I let you get close to me, I fear I will be trapped, engulfed, or smothered.
I must keep my distance from you and not allow you to get close.

UNTANGLING THE KNOT
Closeness can be an exquisite pleasure. As adults, no one can trap, engulf, or smother us. We have our own power to speak, to act, or to leave if we so choose. It is important to be able to be independent, to meet our separate needs. It is also important to be able to be inter-dependent, for the joy of closeness with and support of a caring partner.

THE SCENE

Chris: You know, we seem to be spending less time together. And the only time you touch me is when we make love, which isn't all that often.

Austin: Every time you bring this up, you make me feel like I'm not enough for you. You can take it or leave it, you know. If I'm not enough for you, I'm sorry. Maybe you should be with someone else.

Chris: Thanks a lot.

THE REWRITE

Chris: You know, we seem to be spending less time together. And the only time you touch me is when we make love, which isn't all that often anyway.

Austin: I've started to feel trapped—sort of obligated and smothered, like it's something I have to do.

Chris: You know, if you could just let yourself enjoy me, it might be fun instead of work. You just don't give me much of a chance.

Austin: How about rubbing my neck?

Chris: I'd love to.

23. Pandora's Box

THE LOVE KNOT
If I let you get close to me, you will find out my secrets,
my fears, and how inadequate I really am.
You won't love [respect] me.
I must keep you at a distance.

UNTANGLING THE KNOT
We are all lovable. We are all human. We feel closer
when we can confide our secrets and fears to a caring,
interested partner.

THE SCENE

Frank: It occurred to me recently that you never talk about your previous marriage.

Beth: Nothing to talk about.

Frank: Of course there is. What was your life like then? What happened?

Beth: That was then, this is now. I don't see any point in rehashing it.

THE REWRITE

Frank: How come you never talk about your previous marriage?

Beth: Well, it scares me to talk about it.

Frank: Why?

Beth: Because maybe you'll decide I'm not so great after all. I'm afraid you won't trust me . . . that you might just get up and walk out. . . . You know how I always said that my ex and I just grew apart? Well, he left me after he found out I was having an affair. Pretty tawdry, huh?

Frank: I guess it was hard for you to tell me that. It makes me feel closer to you. Come here . . .

24. Need Knot

THE LOVE KNOT
If I let myself get close to you, I will need you.
If I am too dependent and need (love) you too much, I will not be able to survive without you.
I will lose my ability to be alone, to function on my own.
I will become weak.
I must avoid closeness.
I will distance myself from you, and care less, so that I won't miss [need] you too much when you are gone [die, or leave me].

UNTANGLING THE KNOT
I can enjoy being close to you yet still survive on my own if I need to. As an adult, I am not helpless. I can make a new life for myself if I have to. Meanwhile, the pleasures of intimacy are among life's most fulfilling gifts.

THE SCENE

Red: We have so little time together that I'm getting frustrated.

P.J.: Look, I've got a life away from you, too, you know. I like being with you, but I need my space.

Red: That doesn't leave a lot of room for somebody who loves you and wants to be with you, does it?

THE REWRITE

Red: Why do you insist on our seeing each other just once or twice a week?

P.J.: I don't want to be tied down. I like my independence.

Red: Enjoying each other doesn't mean you lose your independence. It feels good to be close.

P.J.: I guess part of me feels that way. But another part of me is scared to get too close. It'll make me weak. I'll end up needing you too much.

Red: Look, I'm risking that, too. I think we're worth it.

P.J.: You are a pleasure. I guess if I don't risk it, I could lose you, and then I'd never know . . . . So hang in there!

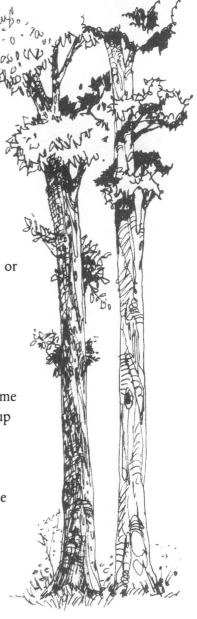

25. Better Safe than Sorry

THE LOVE KNOT
If I love you, I will need you.
I cannot trust you to be there.
Therefore, I cannot [will not] love you.

UNTANGLING THE KNOT
I will decide whether I can trust you based on my actual experiences with you. I will not trust or distrust you based on my history or hidden expectations.

THE SCENE

Tony: I don't think this is going to work out.

Verne: We haven't had time to even see. What's the matter?

Tony: I'm not sure. I just don't have a good feeling about how this will go . . .

THE REWRITE

Tony: I don't think this is going to work out.

Verne: We haven't had time to even see. What's the matter?

Tony: I'm so used to people leaving at the drop of a hat that I'm not sure I can trust you—or anybody else, for that matter.

Verne: You're selling me short. I'm not going to give you up without a fight.

Tony: Well, maybe I'll hang around and see what happens.

26. I Knew It

THE LOVE KNOT
If I love you, I will need you.
I cannot trust you to stay.
I will provoke you, blame you, drive you away.
So when you leave, I will know I was right.

UNTANGLING THE KNOT
I do not create trust by testing you. I will trust you based on my actual experiences with you, and not based on my predictions or past history. Being right in this case is the booby prize. While we are together, I will look to share the joys of closeness, and will stop testing you.

THE SCENE

Sydney: You're an hour late.

Pat: I know, I lost track of time.

Sydney: You've done that a lot lately. In fact, we were supposed to get together Monday and you didn't even call me. Why are you doing this?

Pat: Stop acting like my mother. Maybe I'm late because I'm sick of being nagged to death.

THE REWRITE

Pat: I've been pretty awful to you recently.

Sydney: No kidding, Sherlock.

Pat: I don't blame you for being mad. I'm not really sure why I've been that way. I think I've been testing you, trying to see if you'll put up with me.

Sydney: I'll put up with you, but I won't tolerate intentional thoughtlessness. I feel a lot better now that you've told me what's going on. I was beginning to think you didn't care.

Pat: I think I'm worried about caring too much.

59

27. Ass-u-me

THE LOVE KNOT
If you are distant from me, you don't love me.
Therefore, why should I love you?

UNTANGLING THE KNOT
I will ask and try to understand the reasons for your
distance. I will not assume.

THE SCENE

Toby: I asked you what to do about dinner.

Lou: I'm sorry. I wasn't paying attention.

Toby: That figures. You never pay attention to what I say. Never mind. I'll eat without you.

THE REWRITE

Toby: I asked you what to do about dinner.

Lou: I'm sorry. I wasn't paying attention.

Toby: Yeah. I've noticed that a lot about you lately. What's going on?

Lou: I have a lot on my mind. But it has nothing to do with you. When I finish this project, we'll go out and celebrate. C'mere and give me a hug.

28. Love Me Knot

THE LOVE KNOT

I believe that:

A MAN should never be: *irrational, illogical, weak, passive, sentimental, meek, incompetent, overwhelmed, overwhelming, tearful, wrong, embarrassing* [add your own adjectives of imperfection and inadequacy].

A WOMAN should never be: *demanding, selfish, unfeeling, aggressive, critical, too busy, bossy, angry, rational, embarrassing* [add your own adjectives of imperfection and inadequacy].

If I am these things, I am defective. I must hide, pretend, or wear a mask.

If *you* are these things, you are defective. I feel betrayed. *You broke our contract.* I am entitled to belittle you, deceive you, withhold from you, distance myself from you, not love you.

UNTANGLING THE KNOT

We are all human. We all have moments of frailty, uncertainty, vulnerability, intensity. This does not make us defective. We need to be able to share ourselves with our partners and not hide.

THE SCENE

Madison: I got into another fight with my boss today. That whole thing at work is wearing me out and driving me nuts. I just feel like quitting.

Alex: Why don't you? I really am getting tired of hearing you moan. Every time something happens at work, you come running to me like a kid. I wish you'd grow up.

THE REWRITE

Madison: I got into another fight with my boss today. That whole thing at work is wearing me out. I just feel like quitting.

Alex: Why don't you? I really am getting tired of hearing you moan about it.

Madison: Thanks for being so sympathetic. What the hell's the matter?

Alex: I'm sorry. I had my own problems today. It throws me sometimes, when you talk about giving up.

Madison: You're asking an awful lot if you expect me to let everything roll off my back. You're one of the few people I can talk to.

Alex: I know. It helps just to be able to tell you, though. Keep talking . . .

The Double Binds

The Double Binds

While love knots are unhealthy beliefs that translate into unfair or unrealistic expectations, *double binds* are a heads-I-win, tails-you-lose proposition. They entrap us and our partners because there is no positive way to resolve them. These binds create no-win situations. You are damned if you do and damned if you don't.

If the situation doesn't improve, you usually simply stop trying to please. Or, worse, the situation can be so crazy-making that you begin to doubt yourself and your own senses, constantly feeling inadequate.

Consider this fairly common double bind. "If you give to me, I feel beholden, obligated, burdened. If you don't give to me, I feel unloved, uncared for, unwanted." These are opposing ideas. The only way a person with such a bind will ever be satisfied is to change, to learn to enjoy receiving, to understand that gifts do not have to come wrapped in obligation.

When you find yourself in a double bind, it may help if you tactfully point out the position in which you are placed. Since love knots and double binds usually are not conscious thoughts but attitudes that we act on without thinking, your partner probably will be surprised when you draw attention to them. If you can point out how such a situation affects you, without blaming or attacking, your partner may appreciate the opportunity to make it easier for the relationship to thrive. If your partner displays no interest in changing, you have important information that can help you decide whether this relationship is worth the torment and crazy-making dynamic that double binds inflict on you.

As you encounter double binds, don't despair. Until you recognize the irrational expectations that sabotage relationships, you can't begin to change them. Awareness is a powerful tool. You cannot change destructive attitudes or no-win situations until you know what they are. See how many of the double binds that follow are familiar.

The Double Binds

29. The Single Dilemma

THE DOUBLE BIND

If I am attracted to you, I avoid you, as I am anxious. I believe I am not good enough for you to be attracted to me. If I am not attracted to you, I can be relaxed, at ease, and friendly, as I am not anxious.

I am always with the one I am *not* attracted to.

UNTANGLING THE DOUBLE BIND

I will take the risk of being with whom I am attracted to. My attention and interest are gifts. If they are not accepted, I may be disappointed, but I will survive. And perhaps I will find myself with someone I actually want to be with. Perhaps not. I'll never know unless I risk it.

THE SCENE

Joan: [*Thinks*] Gee, what an attractive guy. For sure, he won't be interested in me. I'm not his type—gorgeous, rich, successful, or thin. Forget it. Ignore him. I'll go talk to that jerk Marvin. Waste of time, but at least he's safe.

THE REWRITE

Joan: [*Thinks*] What a gorgeous guy. Maybe it won't work, but I'm going to talk to him anyway. At least I will have tried. If it doesn't work, I'll be disappointed but I'll survive. If it works, what a blast! [*Says*] Hi!

71

30. Sure You Do

The Double Bind
If you criticize me, I feel inadequate.
If you compliment me, you are placating or trying to control me by saying only what you think I want to hear.

Untangling the Double Bind
I need to be able to listen to, accept, and consider both compliments and criticism. I need to ask for clarification, if needed, and decide what fits. We are all good enough and lovable. We need to be able to trust each other's honesty.

THE SCENE

Rusty: You look great today.

Lee: [*Thinks*] I bet you're just saying this to butter me up. [*Says*] You don't have to judge my appearance every day, you know.

THE REWRITE

Rusty: You look really good today.

Lee: Thank you. I was beginning to wonder. You've spent a lot of time being kinda critical about the way I look.

Rusty: I thought I was being helpful. I was just trying to point out when you looked messy, like when your hair was sticking up. Sorry if I hurt your feelings.

73

31. You Don't Fool Me

THE DOUBLE BIND
If you compliment me, I don't believe you.
I cannot accept compliments.
If you are critical, I do believe you and I feel hurt.

UNTANGLING THE BIND
Honesty is the foundation on which a relationship of
trust is built. When partners are not honest with each
other, they cannot develop trust. And their relationship is
built on the quicksand of deception.
I need to be honest with you about my feelings, wants,
ideas, dislikes, and experiences. And I need to be able to
accept the same from you, both positive and negative.

THE SCENE

Bailey: You look wonderful. I like your new hair style, and that color's great on you.

Alex: [*Thinks*] You never notice how I look. And when *I* say things like that, I'm up to something. [*Says*] What do you want?

Bailey: What do you mean, what do I want? I want you. Come on, gimme a hug!

Alex: Not now. [*Turns away.*]

Bailey: [*Also turns and walks away.*]

THE REWRITE

Bailey: You look beautiful. I like your new hair style, and that color looks great on you.

Alex: Thank you. I love it when you notice. You look pretty good, too.

Bailey: [*Hugging Alex*] I love you.

Alex: I love you, too.

32. Don't Air Your Dirty Linen

THE LOVE KNOT

If I am in pain, I don't tell you, as I believe you would be upset.

When I don't show you my true self, I feel dishonest.

When I feel dishonest, I feel guilty and undesirable. Then I assume that you will find me undesirable and that you would prefer to be with someone else.

I am miserable.

I hate you for making me miserable. I distance from you.

UNTANGLING THE KNOT

Hiding my feelings from you is not a gift. Honest confiding of emotions makes true empathy and bonding possible. If you truly don't want to know my feelings, maybe we shouldn't be together. Confiding is the life blood of an emotionally intimate relationship.

THE SCENE

Ernie: [*Thinks*] I've got a splitting headache.
I'm exhausted. I'm worried about losing my
job. But I can't let on, 'cause Lyn hates it when
I'm no fun.

Lyn: How are you, hon?

Ernie: [*In a monotone, looking morose*] Fine. How
are you?

Lyn: You don't seem fine.

Ernie: [*Abruptly*] I'm fine.

Lyn: [*Thinks*] What's the point of this? [*Says, while
walking out*] See ya later.

THE REWRITE

Ernie: [*Thinks*] I'm glad Lyn will be home soon.
I feel awful.

Lyn: How are you, hon?

Ernie: [*Reaching toward Lyn*] I feel terrible. I've got a
headache and I'm really worried about my job.

Lyn: Come sit by me and tell me about it. Lie down
here, and I'll rub your head. [*Ernie lies down.*] Now,
tell me . . .

77

33. Ton of Bricks

THE DOUBLE BIND
If you need me, I feel obligated, pressured, burdened.
If you don't need me, I believe you don't care.

UNTANGLING THE BIND
Your need does not obligate me. I know that, as an adult,
you have your own strength, resources, and ability to
solve problems.
If you do not need me, it doesn't mean you don't want or
care for me. I can ask and not assume.

THE SCENE

Paige: [*Calling Brooke on the phone*] Hi.

Brooke: [*Thinks*] You've been acting really distant recently, and you haven't really said much about it. I wonder if you've stopped caring about me. [*Says*] Hi.

Paige: I'm glad you're home. I just had a gigantic fight with my dad that ended with him slamming the phone down on me. Can we get together tonight?

Brooke: [*Thinks*] I always feel pressured when you want something from me. [*Says*] I'm sorry. I've already made plans for tonight.

THE REWRITE

Paige: I just had a horrible fight with my dad. He hung up on me. I really need to be with you tonight. Can we get together?

Brooke: [*Thinks*] You sound really rattled. I'm glad you feel like you can depend on me when you need to. [*Says*] Sure. I need to change some plans I made, but I'll be there.

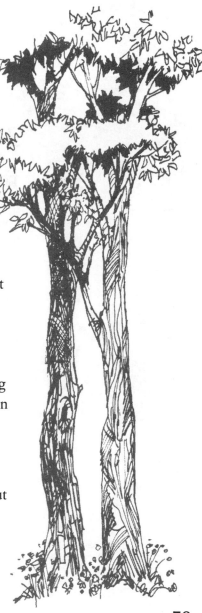

34. If I Have To Tell You . . .

THE DOUBLE BIND

If I tell you what I want and you do what I want, it doesn't count (because I had to tell you).

If I don't tell you what I want, you don't do what I want.

If you do what I want, but not *the way* I wanted you to, it doesn't count.

I feel unloved.

UNTANGLING THE BIND

I cannot expect you to know what I want. Nor can I expect you to do anything exactly the way I would. I can still appreciate the gift of whatever you do because you know I would like it.

THE SCENE

Cal: How come you never call me in the middle of the day anymore?

Ashley: I don't know. I guess I just get busy, and I know I'll see you at night.

Cal: I feel neglected.

Ashley: Well, I'll try to remember to call now and then. I didn't know it meant so much to you.

Cal: Look, don't bother. You've ruined it. It doesn't matter now anyway!

THE REWRITE

Cal: I wish you would call me in the middle of the day now and then, like you used to.

Ashley: I'm sorry. I get so busy I forget, and I guess I just look forward to seeing you in the evening. But I'll call you tomorrow.

Cal: That means a lot. Thanks.

35. Ignorance Is Bliss

THE DOUBLE BIND

If you tell me what you want, I won't do it, because I resent feeling controlled.

If you don't tell me what you want, then I don't know what you want.

What do you want? I'll never know.

UNTANGLING THE DOUBLE BIND

Giving you what you want is an act of caring that nurtures our relationship, pleasures you, and lets you know that I care. I need to be able to do this without feeling controlled or resentful. I can take pleasure in my ability to give.

THE SCENE

Jamie: Could you pick me up at the airport when I get back Saturday?

Casey: Uh, listen, that would really mess up my plans.

Jamie: [*Half joking*] What are you doing that's more important than I am?

Casey: None of your business. You didn't even tell me that you were coming back Saturday!

Jamie: [*Thinks*] Not that it would've made a difference. You're so selfish. [*Says*] Suit yourself.

THE REWRITE

Jamie: Could you pick me up at the airport when I get back Saturday?

Casey: Well, if it's in the morning, sure. I've got plans for the afternoon.

Jamie: Great! My plane's due in at 10:30. Does that work for you?

Casey: Yep. Meet you at the gate?

Jamie: Thanks. I really appreciate it.

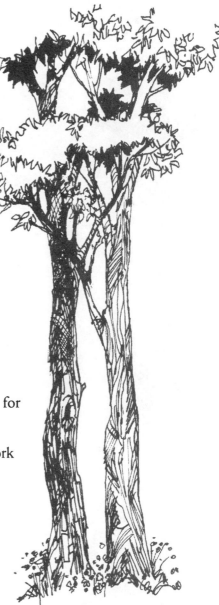

36. Sad Sack

THE DOUBLE BIND

If I tell you what I want, I won't get it.
If I don't tell you what I want, you believe I have
no wants.
You give me nothing. I get nothing.
I am miserable. It's your fault that I am miserable.

UNTANGLING THE DOUBLE BIND

We all have wants. I need to have a time and place when
I can express my wishes, hopes, and dreams. Offering
what each of us wants is part of nurturing our relationship. It is important to respond with attention, affection,
and loving kindnesses.

THE SCENE

Pat: [*Thinks*] I wish we could go out for a really nice evening, but I know you'll say that's wasting money. So why even ask?

Lee: I can finally buy that camera lens I've been wanting.

Pat: [*Says nothing but thinks*] Thanks for thinking of me!

THE REWRITE

Pat: I'd like to go out for a really nice evening with you.

Lee: We'd be spending money with nothing to show for it. I'd rather buy something we can use, like a camera lens.

Pat: Usually I'm okay with that. *This* month, I'd like to go out for a night on the town. It'd give me something to look forward to—something to enjoy *with you*.

Lee: Well, that's fair. [*Moving to embrace Pat*] Thanks for all the times you go along with my ideas.

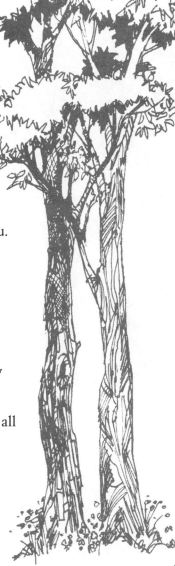

37. Amazing Kreskin, the Mind Reader

THE DOUBLE BIND

If I tell you what I want, you won't do it, as you resent feeling controlled.

If I don't tell you what I want, there's a slim chance you might do it on your own.

So I *never* tell you what I want.

After a while, I even stop letting *myself* know what I want. What do I want? I'm confused.

UNTANGLING THE BIND

If I cannot tell you what I need or want, or how I feel, or what I think, I lose touch with myself. I must find a way to express myself and be able to tell you what I feel and want. If you don't want to know, perhaps we do not belong together.

THE SCENE

Avery: It's hard for me to ask you this. Sometimes I need you just to sit near me and hold me for a while. It seems like something we never have time for any more.

Jan: [*Thinks*] I should have thought of that myself. But maybe you're trying to turn me into some kind of servant. No matter what I do, it's never enough. [*Says*] Not right now, okay? I just feel like being left alone.

Avery: Seems like you've felt like that a lot lately.

Jan: So?

Avery: So nothing. It doesn't matter.

THE REWRITE

Avery: I wish we could take more time to be close and quiet together. I miss you holding me.

Jan: [*Reaches out*] Come here and let me rub your back.

38. Heads You Win, Tails I Lose

THE DOUBLE BIND

If I do what you want, and it's not what I want to do, I resent it.

I believe you would resent it if I do what I want to do (as it isn't what you want to do).

So I *never* do what I want.

I'm miserable. I hate you for making me miserable.

UNTANGLING THE BIND

It is my choice alone and my responsibility to decide what I want to do, whether it pleases you or me. If I choose to do what pleases you, that is my choice. I will take responsibility for my choices in doing things that bring pleasure to my life—whether you join me or not—and not blame you.

The Scene

Tony: What movie do you want to go to
   tonight?

Sandy: [*Thinks*] We go to a movie every Friday
   night. Just once, I wish we could stay home
   and relax. Besides, you always pick those dull
   foreign films, and I always give in. But if I
   say anything, there'll be hell to pay. [*Says*]
   I don't care. Just pick one. [*Thinks*] . . . and I'll
   suffer through it.

The Rewrite

Tony: What movie do you want to go to tonight?

Sandy: Tell you the truth, I'd rather just stay home
   tonight. I feel wrung out. Why don't you go
   tonight, and we can see something else together
   on the weekend?

Tony: Actually, I'd rather spend the evening here
   with you.

39. The Price Is Too High

THE DOUBLE BIND

If I agree to do what you want, and I do it well, you are getting your way.
I resent that.
If I do it badly, I feel less than adequate.
I resent that.
I blame you. It's your fault that I'm upset.

UNTANGLING THE BIND

When I keep my commitments, it is not you getting your way. As an adult, I decide what commitments I make. When I keep them, I am honoring my choices. That is part of being an adult. Commitments allow each of us to know what we can count on. Honoring my commitments builds trust and provides stability in our relationship.

THE SCENE

Kendall: I painted the railing. Do you like
   the color?

Chandler: I thought it was going to be brown.
   I hate orange.

Kendall: I can never do anything right!

THE REWRITE

Kendall: I'm going to paint the railing. Can you live
   with orange?

Chandler: I hate orange!

Kendall: Well, I'll wait until we can agree on a color.
   I don't want to have to do it over.

40. The Good Servant

THE DOUBLE BIND
I work very hard for you to love me. The harder I work,
the wearier I am and the happier you are.
I can't be happy when I am so weary.
I hate you for being happy when I can't be.

If I do what you want, you love me. You only love what
I do . . . not me.
I feel like nothing.
Therefore, I will do nothing.

UNTANGLING THE BIND
As an adult, I am responsible for choosing how much I
want to do. I will not resent you for not feeling the same
way that I do. Nor will I assume that you love me only
for what I do. I will ask when I am in doubt.

THE SCENE

Max: You seem real different lately. All you do is lie around.

Sasha: You sound just like my mother. She was never happy unless I was doing something she wanted.

THE REWRITE

Max: You seem real different lately. All you do is lie around.

Sasha: To tell the truth, I've started to wonder if the real reason you care for me is because I work so hard and do so much.

Max: I love the things you do. Maybe I take that for granted. But don't ever think that's all I love about you. I love you for all kinds of reasons. [*Kisses Sasha and says*] Feel better?

Sasha: Lots.

41. Porcupines

Porcupines draw together for warmth and get stuck on each other's quills.

THE DOUBLE BIND

If I show you how much I love, want, and need you in my life, my desire for you might drive you away. So I *never* show you how much I care.

If I don't show you how much you mean to me and how much I care, you feel unloved. You distance from me.

UNTANGLING THE DOUBLE BIND

Showing love and caring to another is a gift. These feelings do not obligate you, nor need they suffocate you. They are to be appreciated and enjoyed. If you do not appear to welcome my love and caring, then we have important issues to explore and discuss.

42. Gotta Be Me

THE DOUBLE BIND

If I am what you want me to be, I dislike myself.
I resent your wanting me to be what I don't like.

If I am myself, you won't like me.
I resent you for not letting me be myself.

UNTANGLING THE KNOT

You are not responsible for my choices. They are mine
alone. If we cannot work out expectations that we can
both accept and live with, then perhaps our differences
are so great that we shouldn't be together. Perhaps they're
not. We need to be able to talk about them.

43. Hide and Seek

THE DOUBLE BIND
If you try to get close to me, I fear you will trap, engulf, or smother me. I distance.
If you do not try to get close to me, I feel unloved.

UNTANGLING THE DOUBLE BIND
Fear of intimacy deprives us of one of life's greatest pleasures. Knowing that as an adult, I can speak on my own behalf, explore what I need to understand and leave if I wish to, frees me to not have to distance. I can use my power to respond to desires for closeness, yours or mine, in loving ways.

THE SCENE

Ernie: My sister's coming to town. I'm probably going to spend most of the weekend with her.

Lyn: [*Thinks*] Boy, I'm tired of you leaving me alone. [*Says*] Maybe I'll come, too.

Ernie: I'd rather be alone with her.

Lyn: [*Thinks*] You don't want me.

Ernie: I haven't seen her in ages. How about if you and I have Sunday evening together?

Lyn: [*Thinks*] Yeah, and I'll end up feeling so stuck together that I'll be grateful to have to go to work on Monday. [*Says*] Okay.

THE REWRITE

Ernie: My sister's coming to town. I'm probably going to spend most of the weekend with her.

Lyn: Okay.

Ernie: How about if you and I have Sunday evening together?

Lyn: I've got things I want to do most of the evening. How about just dinner?

44. Push Me, Pull You

THE DOUBLE BIND

If I distance from you, I miss what I have with you.
I draw closer.
If I need you, I am weak. I hate myself for being weak.
I resent you for making me weak.
I distance from you.

UNTANGLING THE DOUBLE BIND

Needing others is not a weakness. Each of us must work
on our own history or early decisions that prevent us
from experiencing and filling this need with pleasure.
We all need each other, most certainly for bonding.
Fulfilling this need happily is one of life's greatest
pleasures. We miss it when we don't have it.
When I need you, I don't lose my own strength.

THE SCENE

Len: [*Telephones*] I know I haven't phoned or written, but I think about you a lot! I miss you. I can't wait to see you. Can I see you Sunday?

Chris: This Sunday? I think I can make that. That'd be great!

Len: I may *not* be able to make it. . . . but I'll call you, okay?

THE REWRITE

Len: I know I haven't phoned or written, but I think about you a lot! I miss you. Can I see you Sunday?

Chris: This Sunday? I think I can make that. That'd be great!

Len: [*Facing the discomfort*] The truth is, I think I like you too much. Then I have to check out and see if I can make it without you. Still want to put up with me?

Chris: Let me think about it . . .

45. The Octopus

THE DOUBLE BIND

If you don't love me and stay with me, I will die.
Therefore, I must cling to you no matter what the price.
The more I cling, the more you feel smothered and
lose yourself.
The more you distance, the more I cling.

UNTANGLING THE DOUBLE BIND

As an adult, I have my own power, my own strengths. I
may not want to, but I can survive without you. It is up
to me to develop my resources so I can be self-sufficient
enough not to have to cling.

THE SCENE

Taylor: You were dancing and talking at the party all night to Robin. Are you two having an affair?

Terry: For crying out loud! Robin is married to my partner! How can you be so jealous, so suspicious? I can't go anywhere with you! That's it!

THE REWRITE

Taylor: I need to talk to you about something. I need you to hear me out, okay? [*Terry nods.*] I noticed that you were giving Robin all kinds of attention tonight. I assume that means you were attracted, and I'm wondering if I have anything to worry about. I love you and I trust you. I don't want to cling or be possessive.

I hate feeling this way. I'm frustrated by how often I feel this way.

I appreciate that you *are* very attractive, sexy, and wonderful. I realize that you need to be able to talk to and enjoy other people, but I hope it's me that you love and want the most. Because I love you.

Terry: Thanks for telling me. I had no idea you felt all that. I surely do love you.

46. Strings Attached

THE DOUBLE BIND

If you comfort [give to] me, you are more powerful
than I am.
I will not accept your comfort.
If I comfort you, you are comforted.
I resent you for being comfort-able when I never can be.

UNTANGLING THE KNOT

Accepting comfort from you neither diminishes me nor
empowers you. It is a pleasure to give and receive comfort
from a caring partner. An essential part of intimacy is to
learn to accept and enjoy this.

THE SCENE

Nicky: You look like you had a lousy day.
Why don't I cook dinner tonight?

Sal: [*Thinks*] Then I'll owe you. [*Says*] No thanks,
I'll do it. By the way, is your back still sore?
You want me to rub it for you?

Nicky: That'd be great. It's still bothering me.

Sal: [*Thinks*] You really don't deserve it. [*Says*] Well,
maybe later . . . .

THE REWRITE

Nicky: You look like you had a lousy day. Why don't
I cook dinner tonight?

Sal: I'd like that. You're good at knowing when I
need to be looked after.

103

47. Strangers in a Strange Land

THE DOUBLE BIND

If I were to ask what you are thinking or feeling, I believe I would be intruding (as you would tell me if you wanted me to know).

If I don't ask, you believe I'm not interested, so you never tell me.

We live as strangers.

UNTANGLING THE DOUBLE BIND

Silence does not nurture an intimate bond when that silence is based on a lack of significant information, which is neither offered nor requested. Confiding in each other is the life blood of intimacy. Without it, the relationship withers.

I need to be able to ask for information, and you need to be able to volunteer it when I don't ask, if we are to nurture our relationship. It is crucial that we speak our truths, ask our questions, and keep each other informed.

THE SCENE

Adrian: [*Thinks*] You haven't asked one question about my office meeting today, when they announced bonuses and promotions. Maybe you forgot. Or maybe you're not even interested. Forget it. I won't mention it to you.

Marty: You seem moody.

Adrian: I'm fine. Just drive.

THE REWRITE

Adrian: I got a raise.

Marty: Great! I was afraid to ask.

Adrian: It's okay to ask. I *want* you to want to know what's happening with me. If you don't ask, I think you're not interested. But thanks for being worried—I was, too.

48. Contents Pressurized

THE DOUBLE BIND
If I tell you how I feel, you are angry.
If I don't tell you how I feel, you are angry.
If I tell you how angry I am at you, you distance yourself
from me.
If I don't tell you how angry I am at you, I distance
myself from you.

UNTANGLING THE DOUBLE BIND
We all change with time and new learnings. You and I
need to be able to discuss anything. I need to be able to
tell you my feelings and to know that you will listen with
empathy. I also need to be able to accept and consider
your responses, without assuming I already know what
they will be.

THE SCENE

Allister: [*Thinks*] I'm really sick of your leaving your clothes all over the house. But if I tell you, we'll end up fighting, and the stuff still won't get picked up.

Val: What's the matter?

Allister: Nothing.

Val: Come on, something's wrong. I hate it when you don't tell me what's going on.

Allister: I'm tired of having to pick up after you.

Val: I should've known that's what it was. Boy, are you a nag.

THE REWRITE

Allister: I'm tired of having to pick up after you.

Val: Oh . . . Look, I know it's not your job to pick up after me. I get absent-minded when I get home and drop my stuff in different places. If you'll cut me a little slack when I forget, I'll try to remember to pick it up.

49. Co-Dependency

THE DOUBLE BIND
If I am angry, I cannot tell you, for you would withhold from me, retaliate, or leave.
I am afraid to be without you.
I feel like a coward.
I hate you for making me a coward.

UNTANGLING THE DOUBLE BIND
You cannot make me a coward—or anything. I need to be able to speak my feelings and find out if things can change. I need to tell you how I feel.
And I can survive without you if I have to. Some things are nonnegotiable.

THE SCENE

Gerry: [*Thinks*] It's too much. I'm taking care of cleaning, shopping, and paying the bills. Every time I try to bring this stuff up, Lou either gets angry or says plenty of other people would like it just the way it is. One of these days, I may just let the fool find out! . . . Right. And then what would I do?

THE REWRITE

Gerry: I feel like I'm doing too much around here and that you're not pulling your weight.

Lou: Can't you quit nagging me?

Gerry: I have no intention of nagging you. I'm telling you I'm very unhappy with how things are between us. Something's got to change, and I'm asking you to help me find a way to work this out.

50. Me and My Shadow

THE DOUBLE BIND

If you loved me, you would always want me with you.
If you want to be alone, it means you don't want me
with you.
If you always want me with you, I feel smothered.

UNTANGLING THE BIND

All of us have times when we want to be separate, and
times when we enjoy and want to be together. As adults,
no one can always want to or always be there for another.
We have our separate lives to lead, as well as those parts
we share. These times vary for each of us. We need to be
able to accept these differences and negotiate for the
changes that are important.

THE SCENE

Cal: Look, we need to talk. I'm starting to feel hemmed in, and I need time to myself to sort things out and not feel so pressured.

Billy: I understand how you feel. I'm coming over so we can try to resolve things between us.

Cal: Aargh! I tell you I need time alone, and you insist that we be together? Can't you hear me?

THE REWRITE

Cal: Look, we need to talk. I'm starting to feel hemmed in, and I need time to myself to sort things out and not feel so pressured.

Billy: Well, you've seemed kind of disinterested recently, and maybe I have been pressuring you. I guess I'm afraid of losing you.

Cal: I like being with you, but you make me feel like I *have* to be with you. I feel trapped, not loved. I need to have a choice.

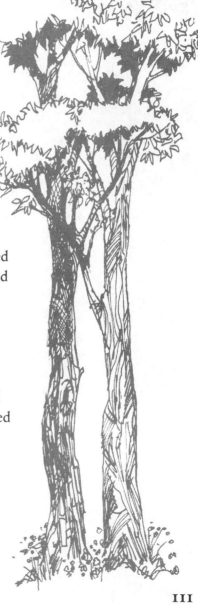

51. Beat It

THE DOUBLE BIND

My commitment to you is too restrictive. I wish to
change it.
I cannot tell you. You would be upset.
To see you is to experience my guilt.
I will find reasons to be angry with you so I need not
feel guilty.
I will provoke you, anger you, drive you away . . .
So I can feel justified in breaking my commitment—
And not feel guilty.

UNTANGLING THE DOUBLE BIND

Relationships change through time. What may have worked at
one time changes as we grow and as our situation changes. My
desire to spend time with others need not be a rejection of
you, but an expression of my own need for variety, new
experiences, and the richness of a range of relationships and
activities in my life. My ability to be separate from you and
enjoy other people and experiences has the possibility to
enrich our relationship.
Neither of us need feel guilty about altering our original
expectations. Without being unilateral or arbitrary, we can
discuss and renegotiate our expectations in an ongoing way.
To maximize mutual pleasure in fulfilling our evolving needs
and goals, our expectations need to encompass change.

THE SCENE

Casey: You really acted like a jerk tonight.

Paige: What are you talking about?

Casey: You always have to be such a know-it-all.
And to top it off, you dressed like a clown.

Paige: Why are you saying this?

Casey: [*Thinks*] I wish I knew. What the hell's the
matter with me? [*Says*] I'm just sick of your
acting like such a spoiled brat.

THE REWRITE

Casey: I love you and don't want to upset you. But
instead of feeling nurtured by our relationship,
I've started to feel trapped.

Paige: How?

Casey: I used to really enjoy going out after work with
people from the office. You got so upset that I
stopped going. But now I've started to lie to you
about having to work late, and I've been slipping out
for a few drinks or for dinner. I've felt mad at you,
and guilty. I've been dealing with it by picking on
you. I want to stop that.

113

And Yet I Love,
Need, Want You . . .

What Now?

❦

U ntangling the love knots and double binds in your life requires special tools. These tools are a combination of knowledge and communication. We cannot communicate effectively if we have only a vague notion of what we want to discuss. And it doesn't help to be able to speak directly or listen fully if we do not understand what is being discussed. Learning to recognize your knots and binds and to "rewrite" them is an enormous first step. Knots and binds create a great deal of havoc. If both partners have them, and they usually do, they interact and grow twisted together and create a unique culture that each partner lives in and contributes to. This section is about how love knots begin, how they ensnare our lovers and ourselves, and how we can talk ourselves out of them.

GETTING STARTED: SOME ORIGINS OF LOVE KNOTS

The human brain is a remarkably complex mechanism that is designed in many ways like a computer. It assures our survival by remembering what is or has ever been a threat to us, so that we can protect ourselves. Beyond threats to our physical survival, it recalls those parts of our unique emotional history that include events or situations that were hurtful or wounding to us. These may be from any time in our life, starting with our earliest beginnings.

An emotionally wounding event or situation is anything that causes distress or deep hurt: sadness, disappointment, fear, grief, rage, resentment, panic.

Whether or not we consciously remember such events, our brain/body memory remembers them. That memory has no sense of time. Even years later, one hint of anything similar to the earlier event can trigger the fullness of our original emotionally intense reaction. This comes to represent what I call an *emotional allergy*.

Physical allergies are related to our immune system having been overwhelmed by too much exposure to a particular substance or chemical. Examples are ragweed for hay fever sufferers, or dander from an animal or pet, or pollen from trees. Later on, even minute amounts of that substance in the air can cause a full-blown allergic reaction, such as wheezing, asthma, hives, itching, or swelling. Sometimes these reactions can be life-threatening, such as when breathing passages threaten to swell shut from the offending substance. Emergency measures might be in order.

Emotional allergy works in much the same way. Consider the story of Ryan, whose parents divorced when he was ten years old. Often left alone at home, he was painfully lonely as a child. Years passed, he went on with his life, and he grew to manhood. He married Rita, a woman to whom he was quickly attracted.

When Ryan returns home at the end of a day, he is eager to be welcomed and greeted warmly. He secretly is hoping and wanting to make up for the painful loneliness and rejection he felt for many years of his life. He wishes Rita would drop everything and show interest in him when he arrives home. When she fails to greet him but disinterestedly continues her chores, he feels hurt, disappointed, and angry. He then punishes her: he "gets even" by coldly ignoring her and by disinterested sullenness.

Rita was raised in a series of foster homes. In her life growing up, the only times she felt accepted, wanted, and appreciated were when she performed household chores quickly and efficiently. She learned to be responsible, to work hard, and to accomplish all her chores quickly and competently. Greetings or gracious gestures of welcome had not mattered to anyone where she grew up, and she long since stopped expecting or expressing affection. She believes that continuing to accomplish her chores responsibly when Ryan arrives home clearly entitles her to his esteem and appreciation.

Both Ryan and Rita have emotionally wounding imprints or memories that deeply affected their decisions in the past—and their expectations in the present. His are from all the years of being left alone, with no one to greet him or to be interested in him when he arrived; hers, from not being valued unless she impressed others with her hard work and single-minded responsibility. Each had made an early decision that was largely out of conscious memory or awareness: "I don't ever want that to happen to me again." Accordingly, they developed emotional allergies. He felt unloved and devalued by Rita's seeming lack of interest and affection upon his arrival home. She felt unappreciated and diminished from his not recognizing how responsible, efficient, and hard-working she was.

THE REVOLVING LEDGER

Each partner invariably hands the other an unwritten ledger of hurts, and desires restitution for this bill, incurred in the past by others. The resulting love knot is: "If you love me, you will know what I need and want, and you will give it to me. You won't hurt me (as I was hurt in the past)." More specifically, Ryan's knot is: "If you love me, you will greet me warmly when I arrive home." Rita's knot is: "If you love me, you will appreciate that I continue to do the chores."

For both, the corollary is: "If you don't do this, I will reject and punish you (and feel justified)."

Their expectations of each other represent reactions to their earlier hurts and disappointments. Inadvertently, they constantly retrigger each other's allergies and negative responses. Rita's lack of attention and affection trigger Ryan's disappointment, which in turn trigger his cold, sullen withdrawal. This triggers Rita's feeling unappreciated and her withdrawal, which again triggers Ryan's anger and coldness.

The Negative Infinity Loop

In situations where both partners trigger each other's allergies, all aspects of their relationship suffer. I call this the *self-perpetuating negative infinity loop*. It continues indefinitely unless the pattern is consciously identified and deliberately changed.

This relationship dynamic is not unusual in couples. I often see this revolving ledger in various forms as I consult in my marriage and family therapy practice. We transfer historical bills to our current partner, in effect saying, *"Make up to me for what went wrong in the past.* Prove to me that you are not like or even similar to whoever hurt me. Otherwise I will punish you—*get even with you—* for what someone else did."

Such ledgers result in the continuing negative infinity loop, complete with unlimited misunderstandings, misperceptions, hurt feelings, and anger in love relationships.

Why Untangling the Knots, Binds, and Loops Is So Hard

Our own knots and binds and the revolving ledger and infinity loop that we have with our partner are an important part of us and of our relationship. They may be nettlesome, even destructive, but they develop out of vulnerability and caring. Knots and binds gain enormous power because they help protect especially tender or wounded places in our hearts. We tend these emotional wounds just as we favor a twisted ankle, being careful not to put too much weight on it or to bump it. In the same way, we often avoid talking about our psychic pains and wounds. This is a love knot in and of itself.

If we do not discuss our deepest hurts and fears, our partners can know nothing about them. Communication—talking *and* listening—about these especially vulnerable areas allows us to build and enjoy the essential ingredient of any relationship: trust.

If communication between partners is filled with chilly silences and raging fights, there is little or no trust. But there are reasons why our ability to communicate is so impaired:

- Most of the things that really matter to us (our basic needs, values, hopes) are wrapped up in or influenced by these relationships.
- Because we "care" about the other person, his or her needs and feelings are also important to us. When they appear to conflict with our own, we're affected much more than we would be if the conflicts arose with a casual acquaintance. Something as subtle as a raised eyebrow, a tightened jaw, silence, or changing the subject can have a powerful negative impact on intimate partners. And we may not even be aware of the cues we are sending.

- Because it is an intimate relationship, we often tend to take things for granted, sending shorthand and sloppy messages.
- We often fall into the trap of thinking that if our partners "really loved" us, they would know what we want or feel without being told.
- Some words, especially those dealing with subjective states and feelings, have many shades of meaning.
- Some experiences and feelings cannot be adequately described by words alone.
- Most of us have often fallen into the habit of using words as weapons (for attack or defense) rather than as tools for sharing information.
- Unless we really *do* know what we're feeling and are prepared to be honest about it, we can unconsciously confuse the issue by sending contradictory messages. Our words may be saying one thing while our tone, facial expression, or body posture says another.

CREATING SHARED MEANING

In enriching a relationship, we first increase self-awareness. The next step is to develop empathy, listening skills, and ways to create shared meaning. Being able to truly understand each other requires dialogue, and half of the dialogue process depends on how the "sender" gets in touch with and transmits perceptions, feelings, expectations, and needs. The other half of the dialogue relies on the "receiver" sharing equal responsibility for ensuring that clear messages are received. This is the part that takes empathy and listening skills.

We seldom if ever really listen to another person except for quite egocentric reasons. We listen to that which is of practical use to us (a film review or a tax loophole), to that which embellishes our own interests or skills (a new tennis grip or a way of preparing no-cholesterol hollandaise sauce), to that which flatters our self-esteem (agrees with our own views), and for plausible opportunities to jump back into the conversation to promote our own opinions. This is quite normal; in fact, humankind might not have survived as a species if we hadn't been so egocentric. But it doesn't promote the kind of empathic listening that permits you to zero in on what the words mean to the speaker, as opposed to the more self-centered value they might have for you.

EMPATHIC LISTENING

True conversation is a partnership in orchestration—not a competition. Pitted against an expert nonlistener, even an articulate speaker becomes dull. On the other hand, an ordinarily inarticulate person, when stimulated and encouraged and reinforced by a true listener, can discover previously unknown depths of feeling and expressiveness. Intimacy grows through this kind of communication.

Empathic listening means focusing on the speaker with an intensity that excludes virtually all other awareness, listening to the thoughts and feelings as well as the words. It means putting yourself in the other person's shoes so thoroughly that you:

- Grasp why the topic is important to that person
- Feel why the speaker chooses each particular word
- Imagine how that person feels in that situation, that mood, and that posture
- Picture what you look like, what signals you are sending, even as the other person speaks

In this way, you begin to appreciate how the words relate to what is going on inside the other person.

Both partners must genuinely want to take in as well as give information; and both of you must do everything in your power, by your manner and tone as well as your words, to facilitate the accurate exchange of honest messages. You must truly want to know what your partner is experiencing, feeling, and needing. If you truly want to know, this will inevitably be reflected in:

- Your manner
- Your concern for each other
- The respect with which you attend to what your partner says
- The way your responses reflect that you have heard and have taken into account what your partner says
- The way you use both your own and your partner's words as tools for illuminating and resolving issues, rather than as weapons
- Your respect for whatever differences emerge rather than being offended or frightened

In short, you show that you really want to know in all the ways that reflect your basic esteem for and trust in both yourself and your partner.

The fact that you are making the effort, are truly listening, shows in a thousand subtle ways that you couldn't possibly program or fake. The tone and pitch of each "uh-huh," the precise wording of each question or comment, and the timing and nuance of each nod, smile, or raised eyebrow tell your partner that you're really grappling to be on the same wavelength.

Since nothing is rarer or more flattering than really being listened to, your partner can't resist the need to be more responsible and honest in formulating and expressing thoughts. It feels good to be listened to, so your partner is far more likely to return the favor when it is your turn to speak.

This kind of communication must be a mutual effort: while one is turning over the loam of their soul and taking risks by sharing what they uncover, the other is showing genuine respect for the speaker and the process by listening with the greatest intensity possible. In so doing, both are showing—and not merely professing—their trust in and respect for each other.

Because both people thereby get in tune with each other's subtleties and complexities of meaning, they avoid making the common mistakes of assuming that they know what the other is or means or wants, and of attributing to the other person their own beliefs and feelings. They both acquire the ability to recognize and appreciate and deal objectively with the differences that exist between them, and from there they can learn how to make these differences occasions for mutual growth and pride rather than divisiveness and fear.

One consequence of genuine communication is that each partner gets in touch with the reality rather than the polite fiction of the other. Truly being known by each other can lead to developing trust, respect, safety in confiding, and an "I-Thou" relationship. No two people are going to have precisely the same wants, needs, values, and beliefs; and these differences make conflict probable. Many differences can be resolved by deeper understanding, adjustments, and compromise. Some may call for mature recognition of the fact that, in a particular area, each person can pursue different ends without harm to the relationship.

THE DIALOGUE GUIDE

The beauty of using the following Dialogue Guide as a tool is that it helps you be very specific about issues that have felt vague. Although it may strike you or your partner as a silly or artificial structure, ask yourself if you are satisfied with the way you currently discuss and deal with touchy issues. Time and again, this guide has contributed to couples' increased understanding of why they are so upset about specific issues and has helped to resolve them.

The Dialogue Guide provides "starter sentences" that may reveal more than you have been aware you were thinking and feeling. Each sentence stem begins with what is called the "I statement." Speaking from this first-person position is less likely to sound blaming than if you start with "You." Many people can listen to and hear "I" statements in a more thoughtful and receptive manner.

The Dialogue Guide can help you confide in your partner in a nonthreatening manner. With some couples, it has profoundly deepened the level of insight and communication.

By way of example, consider the story of Susan and Jim. They have three grown children, all of whom live in different states. Jim is content to stay in touch with occasional letters and visits, restricting long-distance calls to brief, businesslike conversations or problem-solving sessions. But Susan likes to phone each of their children at least every week or two, maybe more often, because it allows her to stay in touch. She can share things—perhaps a joke, a fond memory, or maybe even a tidbit of family gossip.

This drives Jim wild. To him, long-distance calls are for exchanging essential information, not for engaging in unnecessary conversation. When Susan spends more than five or ten minutes on the phone, more likely than not he will begin to pace in the area where she is sitting, glancing at his watch while he fumes.

She may just turn her back to him and try to ignore him, or she might snap, "Just five more minutes!"

After a particularly long call, during which he has spent the last ten to fifteen minutes interrupting and just hovering around, Susan decides to deal with the issue. "Why were you such a pain in the neck while I was on the phone?" she asks.

"Because I can't stand watching you throw money down a rat hole. I have no intention of supporting the telephone company. I swear, I think you do that just to aggravate me."

"Money isn't the issue. You spend more every week on new tools you never use than I do on the phone. I think you resent my being so close to the children. It's not my fault you never tried to keep up with your own kids."

At this point, Jim explodes and makes a counter-accusation, and the argument turns into lengthy antagonism. Or he simply withdraws and refuses to discuss the matter further. Nothing is resolved. Instead, more touchy issues, sore points, and grudges get brought up. Soon, all that is left are open wounds, with no Band-aids® in sight. What starts out as a simple, if cranky, question strays quickly into a number of unrelated areas as each partner tries to outscore the other and to "win."

It might not be easy for Susan and Jim simply to take a look through the love knots in this book and resolve the issues that prompted this argument. Susan and Jim need to talk. They need a way out that is specific to them.

If Susan reads through the list of love knots and double binds, she might discover that one of her hidden assumptions is: "If you loved me, you would know what I want" (in this case, to stay in touch with her kids by phone).

She may also have a rule about anger: "If I tell you how I feel, you will be angry. I am afraid of your anger, so I don't tell you." With these two hidden assumptions, Susan has boxed herself in. Every time she's on the phone for a long time, she ends up feeling unloved, angry, and defensive. When she could take a few minutes to explain why this bothers her so much, she's afraid to, and she decides to skip it. So instead of making her feelings clear, she uses a heated moment to lash out and blame Jim, who lashes back and blames her.

Reading through the love knots can help Susan and Jim gain greater understanding of how certain private rules and beliefs get in the way of their relationship. But they still need to clear things up between them. They need to talk things through in a way that does not obscure the issue with assumptions about each other, concerns about power and who wins the argument, or apprehensions about how the other will respond. This needs to happen in a way that does not threaten each one, and that gives them an opportunity, in turn, to explain clearly and honestly what they think. The realistic expectation in such a conversation is that each will attempt to understand the other, listening carefully with concern and empathy. The goal is to reach a level of positive accord.

The Dialogue Guide provides a structure for such nonthreatening conversations. We are sometimes only vaguely aware of what may be upsetting us, so this guide calls for a deliberate checking out of the major sources of data that influence our reactions in a given situation. It offers starter sentences that are arranged to help you discover and sort out your perceptions, thoughts, and feelings.

Many people are used to expressing thoughts, but not feelings. Some think a thought and a feeling are the same thing. If you have some thoughts or feelings that are pertinent and are not on this guide, feel free to add them. The idea is to share information—to say, in effect: "What I tell you is my truth, and then you can tell me what meaning it has for you and what is your truth."

It is surprising that we often don't even know what we think or feel until we tell someone. People have often reported total astonishment when they realized the range of thoughts and feelings they discovered about what had seemed to be a minor issue.

Your partner's response is not an argument. First it is: "This is what I heard you say," and then it is: "The way it is for me is . . . ." The task for each partner, in turn, is to listen with understanding and empathy. For example, if Susan tried to resolve the issue by using this guide, she might start with something like this:

I NOTICE . . . [*specify the behavior*] that whenever I make a long-distance call, you seem uncomfortable or upset.

I ASSUME THIS MEANS . . .that you don't want me to spend money on long-distance calls.

I WONDER . . . why you feel this way.

I SUSPECT . . . that your concern stems from growing up in poverty, where you learned to do without things that were seen as extravagant.

I BELIEVE . . . that the phone is an important way to maintain close family ties, since our children are spread all over the country.

I RESENT . . . your monitoring my calls and feeling like you are hovering over me whenever I pick up the phone.

I AM PUZZLED BY . . . this being such an important issue for you.

I AM HURT BY . . . your not respecting my decision that this is important to me.

I REGRET . . . even having to talk about this. I believe I have the right to make my own decisions. Keeping in close contact with our children is very important to me. I rarely have time to write letters, so the telephone is my only way. It is not something I do against you.

I AM AFRAID . . . that if you keep doing this, I will make the calls when you are not around and hide them from you. That would make me feel sneaky and guilty and contribute to walls growing between us.

I AM FRUSTRATED BY . . . your not accepting how good it makes me feel to be close to our children.

I AM HAPPIER WHEN . . . you respect my decision about what is important to me. You can decide what is important to you, but I will decide for me. These calls are a nonnegotiable issue for me.

I WANT . . . you to stop hovering over me when I am on the phone, and to accept that it is important to me. I would like to enjoy keeping in close touch with our children.

I EXPECT . . . that this will be hard for you to do or remember.

I APPRECIATE . . . your kindness, sensitivity, and generosity in so many ways.

I REALIZE . . . that it is hard for you to change something that has been ingrained for so long.

I HOPE . . . that you will try to change this, as it is very important to me.

Take a few minutes to review the structure of this Dialogue Guide. Then, with a partner who is willing to experiment with it, set aside half an hour (or more) to practice. Decide who will go first.

To get a feel for using this guide, the "speaker" needs to select an issue. Think of a behavior of your partner or someone else that at times bothers or upsets you. Start with a relatively trivial complaint, such as "I notice that you don't take out the garbage unless I remind you." Pick an issue about which you would like to feel understood by your partner.

Sit comfortably facing each other and in contact by lightly touching each other's hand or foot. It's harder to misunderstand each other when we're in touch. Remember, the information is to be conveyed and reflected in a low-key, nonargumentative fashion. Both of you are simply trying to share information.

As the speaker begins, the other person should just listen—listen to what's being said with empathy and interest, and to increase your understanding. Do not interrupt with advice, rebuttal, judgments, or comment.

At the end of each step ("I notice" starts the first step), the listener repeats or mirrors back what he or she heard. If you can restate someone else's thoughts and feelings accurately, you create *shared meaning*. For the "listener," the point is that your partner is confiding in you; and you are validating that confidence by listening, clarifying, and accurately restating what you heard. To show your appreciation for being taken into confidence, you may at times want to offer a gesture such as a thank-you with a hug or a kiss.

As listener, your role is to understand what your partner is saying, not to add information or "correct" the story in any way. For the sake of remembering or complete clarity, you can stop your partner after one or more sentences and repeat what you just heard. Whatever you may have misheard or misunderstood, your partner can then restate and clarify. Then you state your new understanding. This continues until your partner verifies that your restatement is completely accurate. You can ask, "Is that it?" or "Do I have it?"

This step is essential before you go on to take your turn, in which you can either respond to your partner's issue or raise one of your own.

After the second partner finishes, hold a general critique. Evaluate both the process and the substance. The *process* refers to how it felt for each of you to give and hear the self-disclosure, how it felt to be confided in. In this context, the *substance* means the degree to which you exchanged new information or better understood certain issues. It is interesting to share how using the guide may have put you in touch with feelings and thoughts that perhaps neither of you realized you had.

This guide is merely a model, a reminder that these various thoughts and feelings exist and affect our expectations and behaviors. You can, when you choose, become aware of these expectations so as to have a broader base of understanding with each other.

As you grow more comfortable and familiar with a sequence of observations and feelings, you may want to tailor it to your own needs.

DIALOGUE GUIDE

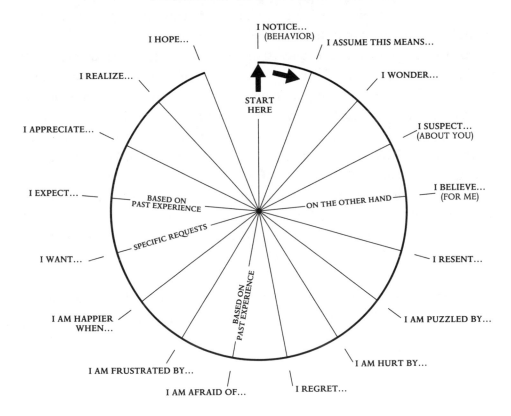

You can change the order of sentences and subtract or perhaps add your own sentence stems. You may want to ask: "How does this feel for you?" or "How can we work this out?" However, it won't do you any harm to practice the Dialogue Guide for a while in the sequence suggested. Everything in the sequence can be of value in developing deeper levels of understanding for yourself and your partner. It can even be of help in simply reviewing for yourself your own thoughts and feelings at any particular time.

When you sense that you're getting into an uncomfortable issue area, one in which potential conflict or misunderstanding exists, a conscious effort to check all the points on the Dialogue Guide can save both of you time and grief.

While the Dialogue Guide illuminates a range of facets that may sabotage your relationship—and helps resolve them—the next exercise takes the dialogue to a deeper level of confiding and even deeper levels of understanding and empathy with your partner.

The Price We Pay

Great communication means two people confiding and listening to each other with empathy. The following exercise can help you understand the part your unique personal history played in developing your expectations. It can provide answers that both you and your partner can use to disengage from the stuckness of the *negative infinity loop*. Here are the steps:

1. As the sender, tell your partner which knot you want to work on. Tell why this knot [or bind] exists, where in your life this belief came from.
2. The receiver's role is to create shared meaning, asking for clarification as needed.
3. The sender then reflects on and describes "The price I've paid in my life for this knot—in my feelings, thoughts, behavior, and relationships." Reflect on and describe "The price that I believe you, my partner, has paid for my having this knot."
4. The receiver responds with shared meaning.
5. The sender reflects on and describes "What do I really want that this knot was designed to achieve? Why did I develop it? How did I believe it would serve me?"
6. The receiver responds with shared meaning.
7. Using "I" statements (I feel . . . , I believe . . . , I choose . . . , etc.), the sender reflects on and describes "What do I need to do to unravel this

knot—in my thoughts, feelings, and behavior?" and "What can you, my partner, do to help me in this plan?"

8. The receiver continues to respond with shared meaning and can then reflect on the request, accept it, or accept it with conditions.

9. The sender reflects shared meaning.

10. Both partners arrive at a commitment to act based on the information shared and the issue to be resolved. The session concludes with mutual thank-yous and messages of appreciation for being confided in, and for being listened to with sensitivity and accuracy.

With the list of love knots and binds as a Road Map, and the Dialogue Guide or Price We Pay exercises as a compass, you have new tools to use with your partner for resolving conflicts. They can help you identify some of each other's personal assumptions and beliefs and how they may be causing problems that neither of you need.

By acknowledging some of the silly or damaging things we have believed, and the things we do, we can laugh at them together. Confiding in a loving, empathic partner who wants to understand helps us not only to understand ourselves but also to change those feelings and behaviors that sabotage the pleasure possible between intimates. Then, in an air of mutual trust and honesty, we can replace them with more livable, human beliefs that allow those we love to know what we want or expect—and give them and ourselves a fair chance to meet these more realistic expectations.

Hidden Expectations Checklist

Use the following list to discover some of your own hidden expectations. Read through it and check the beliefs that are true for you. Put a question mark next to any that you suspect may be true for your partner. Then, when you can, set aside a time to read through the list together for clarification and discussion. You can use the Dialogue Guide to get a deeper level of understanding and resolution. You can use the "Shared Meaning" exercise to feel really heard and understood. And you can use the "Price We Pay" exercise to clarify for yourself and your partner the origins of your distress and how you can change it.

IF YOU LOVED ME . . .

☐ You would listen to me.
☐ You wouldn't interrupt me.
☐ You would pay attention to me.
☐ You would talk to me.
☐ You would care about me and show it.
☐ You would do things for me.
☐ You would do the things I ask you to do.
☐ You would help me.
☐ You would appreciate me and tell me so.
☐ You would stand up for me when someone criticizes me.
☐ You would take my side.

□ You would encourage me.

□ You wouldn't tell me what to do.

□ You wouldn't nag me.

□ You would be happy to see me and be with me.

□ You would want to be with me.

□ You would spend time with me.

□ You would put time with me ahead of spending time with other people.

□ You would do the things I like to do.

□ You wouldn't complain.

□ You would keep your word.

□ You would never lie to me or deceive me.

□ You would never ignore my feelings.

□ You would never belittle me.

□ You would pick up your socks and dirty clothes.

□ You would tell me that you love me.

You can add your own hidden expectations here . . . as well as those you suspect are true for your partner.

Keeping Current

The Daily Temperature Reading

. . . love does not just begin when the lights go out. Love is a daily ongoing experience, nourished or starved out, depending upon its care and feeding. It flourishes on little things . . . a touch, a secret shared, a meal prepared together, a song written . . . . These are the things that love can live on. Touch the heart and all the rest will flow.

—*Elisa Brown,* How Can I Show That I Love You

I present here a final major format for keeping current with each other, nurturing your relationship, and avoiding future knots and double binds. It is in effect like watering a garden. Virginia Satir introduced me to this idea of the daily temperature reading, which is a way to connect with each other and to stay abreast of changes. In PAIRS, we use it as a way to prevent misunderstandings from developing in the future. Graduates of our course tell me two things: that it is one of the most important techniques they have for staying close and current, and that all too often when they get busy, they let it slide.

Don't let it slide.

In relationships that thrive, people make time to be alone together and to confide what is on their minds and in their hearts. If that isn't familiar for you, the Temperature Reading may seem artificial or clumsy at first. Be aware of its importance and make a decision to do it—as with a savings account. Take the time off the top of your schedule regularly. This is like an insurance policy on your relationship to keep it current and to sustain it as a source of pleasure.

To take a Daily Temperature Reading with each other, the format for keeping up to date is:

1. **Appreciation**
2. **New information**
3. **Puzzles**
4. **Complaints with requests for change**
5. **Wishes, hopes, and dreams**

You don't have to cover all five areas every day, but consider whether you have something to say in an area; if you do, say it.

APPRECIATION

We are all vulnerable. We all need to be recognized and to know what's good about us, and nobody is better equipped to tell us this than the person who is closest to us. Whatever you appreciate about your partner, let him or her know. We hear so much about what's *wrong* with us. The world tells us, and we tell ourselves all the time; we're usually our own worst critics. When you recognize qualities in your partner that you appreciate, express it—with words or with a gesture, but express it.

Hearing and receiving appreciation regularly is an important element in nurturing our self-esteem. Self-esteem need not come only from outside ourselves, but feeling appreciated, loved, and accepted by our partners helps us to thrive. Feeling loved is one of the most important areas of fulfillment in life It is also important to know what we are appreciated for; *and* we have to learn to *listen* to our partner's appreciation and take it in. Too many of us have a conditioned pattern of pooh-poohing compliments ("Oh, this old thing?" or "It was nothing") and then feel unrecognized and unappreciated.

NEW INFORMATION

So much of what goes wrong in relationships is because we do not have the information we need to understand what's going on. Not knowing leaves too much room for assumptions—often faulty ones. Intimacy thrives when both partners know what is happening in each other's life. It may be related to work ("I'll be in Boston overnight on Monday"), family news ("Mom is lonely and she's coming to visit"), fears and worries, or interests—anything and everything, trivial and important, that helps keep your partner informed on your state, mood, and what's going on in your life generally. It can even be what you dreamed last night.

PUZZLES

Another breeding ground for false assumptions is confusion or puzzlement. If there are things you don't understand, ask your partner for clarification.

"Who was that on the phone?"

"Why did you come to bed so late last night?"

"Why did you seem so edgy this morning?"

Avoid mind reading, and don't assume your partner can tell what you want to know.

This step of the Daily Temperature Reading is also a chance to delve into any puzzles you may have about yourself.

"I'm not sure why I'm having so much trouble concentrating today. This isn't like me."

"You know, when I got so mad at that driver who pulled out in front of me, I don't know what was going on. It feels important somehow."

You may not suddenly get all the answers you want, but you do give your partner a chance to see more of your inner life—your thoughts, your struggles, your worries. Sometimes this can lead to insight (by you and your partner), sometimes to relief. Your partner may find out that your preoccupied mood has nothing to do with the relationship, and you get to share something meaningful.

COMPLAINTS WITH REQUESTS FOR CHANGE

This step of talking about complaints is designed to provide information, not to be blaming or judgmental. When you state your complaint, be specific about which behavior displeases you, and state which behavior you are asking for instead (what the solution is), e.g.: "I resent it when you take me to your office party and don't introduce me to anyone. I need you to introduce me to people so I don't feel like such a stranger."

You can use the Dialogue Guide to resolve an issue, or you can request a Fair Fight for Change if you think you need a lengthier structure (refer to my book *Passage to Intimacy* for information on how to have a Fair Fight). Or you can simply say, "This thing happened that bothered me, and I would feel better if you would do this other thing instead."

This book presents 51 knots and binds, so you might choose to include one a week in this part of your Daily Temperature Reading. By working on and resolving these issues in a systematic way, you can keep erroneous beliefs or assumptions from sabotaging your most cherished relationship.

Information, puzzles, and complaints are all part of solving problems. The idea is to provide information that will bring you and your partner closer. Romance may thrive on mystery, but intimacy doesn't.

WISHES, HOPES, AND DREAMS

Amidst the bustle of modern life, many couples stop confiding their dreams once they pass through courtship. Careers, home life, social calendars, and other pursuits often push aside the seemingly "dispensable" pleasures of sharing our yearnings and aspirations for the future. Unfortunately, this deprives us of some of the most exquisite and nourishing energy we can find in intimacy.

For others, sharing hopes and dreams doesn't even happen during courtship. If I have rules that say I shouldn't let myself know what I'm thinking or feeling or wanting—much less let you know—then it's almost impossible to sustain a comfortable, close relationship. Our hopes and dreams are integral, vital parts of who and what we are. If we don't share them with our partners as information (not demands or complaints), we deprive the relationship of tender, vulnerable parts of ourselves.

Reflecting on, recognizing, and sharing our dreams does three things. It adds to our self-awareness, it nurtures our relationship, and it increases the possibility that we will find a way to realize our dreams.

The point is not to judge our dreams (or each other's) or their likelihood, but to develop the kind of closeness and trust that lets us feel safe sharing whatever we experience. Dreams and longings range from the ordinary to the extraordinary:

"I wish I'd win the lottery."
"I wish that loud neighbor would move!"
"I wish people at work were friendlier."
"All my life, I've wanted a huge family—a whole bunch of kids."
"I wish we could get away this weekend."
"I fantasize about sailing around the world some day."
"I'd like to try that new Thai restaurant."

The Temperature Reading is like watering the garden of your relationship. If you fail to do it, ask yourself why. At times, you may feel less eager to do this updating, less likely to take the time with your partner. Sometimes we are so upset that we don't want to share our thoughts with our partner. When feelings are running that strong, just holding each other may be more appropriate. Many couples do the Temperature Reading while they are snuggling. Some even do it long-distance: on the telephone, in a letter, or by E-mail.

Sometimes we may neglect sharing our longings because we fear being rejected, or having our dreams ridiculed. At such times, it helps to *talk about that fear* before talking about our hopes and wishes. If your wishes or expectations or hopes are different from mine, it doesn't make one of us noble and the other ignoble. It just means that we are all different and, in being different, we have different dreams and expectations. The more we can bring these into our awareness and talk about them, the higher the possibility that we will reach some accord.

Martin Buber, in his classic work *I and Thou,* says that when two people can be with each other without any masks, without pretense, without hiding, it is one of the most vitalizing experiences in life. Treating your partner not as an object but as a cherished other to honor, respect, trust, and confide in, and from whom you don't have to hide your true self, increases your flow of energy, your self-worth, and your sense of closeness and safety in the world.

Epilogue

❧

This book is a relationship detective and puzzle-doer. It presents aspects of my discoveries regarding nurturing and sustaining loving relationships, along with beliefs and behaviors that sabotage intimacy. If this little volume speaks to you, you may wish to experience other parts of my exploring. Many of them are detailed in my book *Passage to Intimacy* (contact Science and Behavior Books, Inc., 1-800-547-9982), which offers key concepts and skills from my PAIRS program.

PAIRS is a semester-long program on the Practical Application of Intimate Relationships Skills. (For a fuller description, see the Introduction.) Internationally recognized as the most comprehensive, uniquely effective course in the field today, it offers a carefully sequenced series of lectures and dynamic experiential exercises. These provide opportunities to develop new perceptions and skills, to learn from other group members, and to share with your partner in far greater depth. It provides a model for an I-Thou relationship. By practicing the skills you gain in PAIRS, you can create a foundation that sustains a cherished love relationship—a foundation that will support personal growth, healing, transformation, and empowerment.

If you would like more information or wish to participate in a class, trained leaders are actively teaching the PAIRS program in the following locations.

UNITED STATES OF AMERICA
Alaska: Fairbanks: Vincent Gologly, Ph.D.; Bruce Hill, Ph.D.: 907-451-7270
Arkansas: Little Rock: Jean Speegle, LCSW: 501-663-4723
California
Encino: Lillian Klempfner, Ph.D.: 818-906-7781
Encino: Francine Ticknor, Psy.D.: 818-990-0031
Los Angeles: Nili Shalev, Ph.D.: 310-247-0800
Los Gatos: Joan Crawford Anderson, MSW: 408-429-7467
Colorado
Boulder: Barbara Moss, M.S.; Shelly Moss, MSW: 303-444-9640
Boulder: Michael Moore; Robin Temple, M.A.: 303-786-8662
Connecticut
New Haven: Barbara Kahn, M.S.; Howard Kahn, Ph.D.: 203-624-9411
Trumbull: Nora Gluck, CISW; Jeffrey Blum, Ph.D.: 203-686-6227
Florida
Fort Lauderdale: Ellen Haag; Gregory Haag, M.D.: 305-434-9191
Fort Myers: Sharon Tobler, Ph.D.: 941-336-7464
Miami: Phyliss Koss, MSW: 305-595-5677
Tampa: Janet Salyers, M.A.: 613-932-8999
Hawaii: Kihei, Maui: John Tyler, J.D.; Natalie Garber Tyler, Ph.D.: 808-879-0097
Illinois
Chicago: Bud Baldwin, M.D.; Michele Baldwin, Ph.D.: 312-337-0506
East Dundee: Marsha Bonham, M.S.: 708-610-4278
Indiana: Granger: Barbara Seldin, Ph.D.; Fredric Seldin, Ph.D.: 219-272-3723
Iowa: Iowa City: Nell (Ann) Penick, Ph.D.: 319-337-3087

Louisiana: Covington: Paula Norris, M.Ed.: 504-835-1244

DeRidder: Pamela Evans: 318-531-1938

New Orleans: Jesse Adams, J.D.; Teresa Adams, ACSW: 604-568-1107

Maryland

Bethesda: Frank Doyle, Ph.D.; Bonnie Eisenberg, Ph.D.: 301-652-3730

Lanham: Kevin Barwick, M.A.: 301-672-1911

Massachusetts

Cambridge: Bunny Duhl, Ph.D.: 617-547-6677

Hampden: Joseph P. Costanzo, Ed.D.: 413-566-8503

Missouri: St. Louis: Meg Haycraft, MSW: 314-993-1940

New Jersey

East Windsor: Linda M. Kibrick, MSW, ACSW; Bill Rhoads, MSW, ACSW: 609-448-7333

South Orange: Sonya Aronson, MSW; Ted Aronson, MSW: 201-763-4116

South Orange: Elaine Braff, MPS, ATR; Hal Braff, J.D.: 201-763-0181

New Mexico: Santa Fe: Shanti Elke Bannwart, M.A.; Claude Phipps, Ph.D.: 505-583-2141

New York

New York: Carolyn Perla, Ph.D.: 212-769-1837

New York: Clifford Sager, M.D.: 212-288-1238

North Carolina

Cary: Don Adams, Ph.D.; Jo Adams, R.N.; Don Azevedo, Ph.D.; Janice Azevedo, MSW; Dick Stern, M.E.; Ruth Russell-Stern, Ph.D.: 819-469-0864

Hazelwood: (Summers only): Greg and Ellen Haag: 704-452-1550

Waynesville: Beverlee Marks Taub, Ph.D.: 704-456-7220

Ohio: Beavercreek: Sharon Trekell, M.S.: 513-435-1472

Oregon: Corvallis: Tim Barraud, LMT; Linda Carroll, M.S.: 503-758-4118

Pennsylvania

Bala Cynwyd: Judith Temple Jackson, Ph.D.; Moss Jackson, Ph.D.: 610-642-4872

Gwynedd Valley: Rita DeMaria, M.S., Ph.D. (cand.): 215-628-2450

South Carolina: Mount Pleasant: Rebecca Denslow, MSW: 803-881-4228

Texas: Houston: Nancy White, Ph.D.: 713-961-5243

Virginia

Alexandria: Peggy Errington, Ph.D.; Joe Sanders, Ph.D.: 703-543-3666

Alexandria: Ann Ladd, Ph.D.: 703-998-5233

Fairfax: Frank Roberts, LCSW: 703-323-5233

Falls Church: Carlos Durana, LPC, Ph.D.; Lane Franz, Ph.D. Candidate; Paul Franz; Judy Hurvitz, MSW; Peter Schroeder, MSW; Suzanne Scurlock; Lynn Turner, LCSW, Ph.D.; Chris Wright, M.A.: 703-998-0300

Falls Church: Michele Goss, Ph.D.; Norman Jones, M.A.: 703-996-6570

Falls Church: Rev. Carl L. Nissen, STD: 703-532-6518

Norfolk: Jeff Karako, MSW; Suzanne Karako, MSW: 804-427-8392

Norfolk: Bonnie Rabinowitz, LCSW; Marc Rabinowitz, LCSW: 604-822-9852

Roanoke: Audra Seagle, Ph.D.: 703-772-1872

Washington: Bellevue: Carol E. Wright, M.A., MFT; James A. Wright, B.S., R.C.: 206-454-2262

Wisconsin: Milwaukee: Naomi Cohn, MSW; Eric J. Ehrke, MSW; Onnolee Stevens, MSW: 414-278-7980

AUSTRALIA: Parkside/Adelaide: Dr. Stefan Neszpor, FRCPC: 8-364-0882

CANADA

Alberta: Calgary: Sig Taylor, MSW: 403-528-5600 or 529-8966

British Columbia

Surrey: Bill Dyck, M.A.; Charlotte Dyck, M.A.: 604-272-4255

Vancouver: Douglas Adams, MSW; Lanalee Cleveland-Schmidt, Ph.D.: 604-574-5178

Ontario

Cookstown: Joyce Cornish, M.Ed.: 705-456-2135

Duntroon: Lynda Rees, R.N., B.A., M.Sc.: 705-444-7682

London: Marlene Rees-Newton, MSW: 519-646-6100 ext. 5978

Saskatchewan: Saskatoon: 306-652-0934: Myra McPhail, BsoN, Ed.CCV

ENGLAND

London: Paul Alsop, MSW; Terry Cooper; Oriel Methuen; Jenner Roth, MSW:
81-341-2277

FRANCE

Paris: Jill Bourdais, MSW: 1-4354-7925

Paris: Judith Collignon, MSW: 1-4027-8775

ISRAEL

Givataim: Yardena Arnon, MSW: 03-571-9173

Karma Yossef: Haya Yaniv, RN; Yehuda Yaniv: 06-242-539

Natanya: Zev Appel, MSW, Ph.D.: 05-366-837

Ramat Hasharoa: Claire Rabin, Ph.D.; Yossi Rabin: 03-540-3031

As the training and locations continue to expand, you may wish to call the PAIRS offices at 1-800-477-2477 for the location of current classes.

The PAIRS Foundation was established in 1984 and is a nonprofit, nonsectarian, educational corporation. Developed to design programs for the prevention of relationship breakdown, it is now applauded internationally by therapists and participants alike. In addition to the PAIRS program, the Foundation offers the following direct services.

- Workshops and classes for couples
- Workshops and classes for individuals
- Lectures on relationship issues for the general public
- Referrals for couples and individuals
- Literature, video- and audiocassettes
- Leader training for mental health professionals

I welcome ideas about new knots or binds, particularly those that are specific to single adults, adolescents, children, the corporate world, and the workplace. If you have new knots or binds to add to my list, or for further information, please write me at:

PAIRS International, Ltd.
3705 S. George Mason Drive, Suite C8
Falls Church, VA 22041

telephone: 1-703-998-5550
fax: 1-703-998-8517

I hope that the understandings and the exercises in this little volume have helped and will continue to help you in avoiding the pitfalls that so often sabotage loving relationships. I hope they will help you to create and sustain the love in relationships that you truly wish for.

Other books from Science & Behavior

Passage To Intimacy   12.95 QPB
by Lori H. Gordon, Ph.D.

Based on the key concepts and skills from Lori Gordon's Heralded PAIRS (Practical Application of Intimate Relationship Skills) program, *Passage to Intimacy* emphasizes concrete, substantive techniques that make a difference in the quality of a couple's life together. Gordon identifies three hopes and three fears that determine the path to intimacy for each of us, offers a framework for guidance through the illustrative Relationship Road Map and provides the PAIRS tool kit for solving problems.

New Peoplemaking   19.95 QPB
by Virginia Satir

Revised and expanded seminal work on families, with over a million copies sold in 12 languages. It expresses her most evolved thoughts on self-worth, communication, family systems, and the ways people relate to each other.

Satir Step-by-Step   16.95 QPB
A Guide to Creating Change in Families, by Michele Baldwin & Virginia Satir

Annotated transcripts of Satir doing family therapy—showing what she is thinking and how she selects a particular phrase or intervention—and then an account of her theoretical foundations and methods.

Conjoint Family Therapy   17.95 QPB
by Virginia Satir

Third edition of this universally recognized classic in family therapy. In the introduction Satir writes, "I offer this book as a conceptual frame around which to organize your data and your impressions, rather than something to be memorized . . . a suggested path."

Meditations of Virginia Satir   10.95 QPB

Peace Within, Peace Between, Peace Among, by Anne Banmen & John Banmen

A compilation of Virginia's meditations and essays that illuminate and guide readers on the complex interplay of mind, body, emotions, and spirit. Presented in a series of short, highly readable meditations for use individually or with groups.

The Satir Model   23.95 hardcover

Family Therapy and Beyond, by Virginia Satir, John Banmen,
   Maria Gomori & Jane Gerber

The most definitive book on the theoretical aspects of Satir's approach to therapy. Comprehensive organization of her concepts, therapeutic applications, and innovative interventions. Winner of the AAMFT 1984 award for Satir research.

Family Reconstruction   19.95 QPB

The Living Theater Model, by Sharon Wegscheider-Cruse, Kathy Higby,
   Ted Klonyz & Ann Rainey

Family Reconstruction is an active and dramatic therapy tool created by Virginia Satir to help people reclaim freedom of choice and self-worth. The living theater model of family reconstruction seeks to reframe current thinking in order to promote a bigger picture of reality, to increase self-worth, to break the power of compulsive behavior in order to provide freedom of choice, and to develop safe and useful relationship skills.

New from Science & Behavior

Grandparenting   14.95 QPB

by Sharon Wegscheider-Cruse

Inspired by the transformation that occurred in her life after the birth of her first grandchild, Wegscheider-Cruse shares her experiences as a loving grandmother and a family therapist of 25 years. Playfully illustrated and easy to read, *Grandparenting* explores the joys and difficult issues associated with grandparenting today, including over 50 activities designed to enrich the bond between grandparent and grandchild. This is a perfect book for any grandparent, foster grandparent, aunt, uncle, neighbor, or friend who plays a grand "role" in a child's life.

ORDER FORM

Tear out and mail this form to:

Science & Behavior Books, Inc.

2225 Grant Road, Suite #3
Los Altos, CA 94024

Please Send Me:

____ copies of *Passage To Intimacy*	$12.95	$ _____
____ copies of *New Peoplemaking*	$19.95	$ _____
____ copies of *Satir Step by Step*	$16.95	$ _____
____ copies of *Conjoint Family Therapy*	$17.95	$ _____
____ copies of *Meditatons of Virginia Satir*	$10.95	$ _____
____ copies of *The Satir Model*	$23.95	$ _____
____ copies of *Family Reconstruction*	$19.95	$ _____
____ copies of *Grandparenting*	$14.95	$ _____
Tax (add 7.75% for CA residents)		$ _____
Freight & Handling ($3 first book, $1 each add'l)		$ _____
Total Amount Enclosed		$ _____

☐ *Please send me a free catalog.*

Name: _____

Address:_____

City: _____ State: _____ Zip: _____

Phone: (___)_____

Charge to my credit card: Visa: ☐   MasterCard ☐

CC#:_____

Expiration Date:_____

Signature: _____

Phone (800) 547-9982 or Fax (415) 965-8998